Adorable
Crochet
for Babies
and Toddlers

Adorable
Crochet
for Babies
and Toddlers

Lesley Stanfield

COLLINS & BROWN

Contents

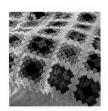

INTRODUCTION

Crochet has a lot to recommend it. As well as being quick, easy and very portable, it offers endless scope for shaping, adding embellishments and playing with colour. I have tried to encapsulate all these qualities in this collection.

Clothes for babies and toddlers are fairly quick to make, if only because of their small size, and those made in crochet can take very little time indeed. Designed to be stylish and comfortable, all these projects are either fairly simple or very simple, using no complex stitch patterns. Wherever possible, clothes and toys are made in the round to minimize sewing up and to exploit the character of crochet. Explanations of techniques are included so that this book can be used by beginners and by those whose crochet skills are a little rusty. Very few stitches need to be mastered, and these are all closely related to each other.

Besides clothes, designs for toys and blankets are included. The toys should become nursery favourites, while the blankets and covers will make wonderful throws long after the baby has outgrown them. Both small-scale and large-scale, the designs include ideas for gifts as well as essentials.

As choice of yarn and colour is all-important, the designs have been grouped by colour. This doesn't mean that the designs won't work equally well in other colours, it's simply to emphasize how critical this ingredient is. So enjoy selecting colours and planning your project, creating it, and finally basking in the satisfaction of completing it.

CROCHET BASICS

MATERIALS

CROCHET HOOKS

Very fine crochet hooks are usually made of steel, medium-size hooks are aluminium and very large hooks may be plastic to reduce their weight. The hook should have a smooth, undamaged point and be light and comfortable to use.

YARNS

All kinds of yarn can be used for crochet, although highly textured yarns can be difficult to work with. Heavyweight yarns are unsuitable as they make a very thick fabric, even if worked in an open stitch. The best yarns are those which run smoothly and don't split easily.

Most of the projects in this book specify the brand and type of yarn to be used. The exceptions are the patchwork items and some small accessories which use oddments of yarn. To achieve the best results it's advisable to use the specified yarn. However, if substitution is unavoidable try to match the thickness and generic type of yarn – for example, 4-ply or Double Knitting. This will enable you to work to the correct tension and therefore make a garment the intended size. Assessing the quantity of yarn needed is trickier because, although two yarns may be a similar thickness, they may be very different in length, depending on the fibre content and composition. A 50g ball of yarn manufactured from man-made fibre could be expected to have a greater yardage than, say, a 50g ball of cotton. The length of yarn in the ball is usually stated along with weight on the ball band. With this information it should be possible to calculate the approximate amount needed for a particular design.

Crochet Hook Conversion Table

Metric sizes (I. S. R.)	0.60 mm	0.75 mm	1.00 mm	1.25 mm	1.50 mm	1.75 mm	2.00 mm	2.50 mm	3.00 mm	3.50 mm	4.00 mm	4.50 mm	5.00 mm	5.50 mm	6.00 m m	7.00 mm	8.00 mm	9.00 mm	10.00 mm
Old U.K. (wool)							14	12, 13	10, 11	9	8	7	6	5	4	2, 3	0, 1	000, 00	
Old U.K. (cotton)	7, 7½, 8	6½	5½, 6	4 ½, 5	3½, 4	2½, 3	1½, 2	0, 1	3/0, 2/0										
U.S. (regular/ jumbo/ jiffy/ afghan)								1	2	3, 4	5	6	7	8	9	10, 10½	11, 12	13, 15	
U.S. (regular/ jumbo/ jiffy/ afghan)								B	C	D, E	F	G	–	H	I	J, K			
U.S. steel	14	13	11, 12	9, 10	8, 7	6	4, 5	1, 2, 3	0										

FIRST STEPS

What follows is for guidance only, as there are many ways to handle hook and yarn. These explanations are for right-handed people; anyone who is left-handed will need to reverse the diagrams, either by reflecting them in a mirror or by tracing them and then turning over the tracing paper.

HOLDING THE CROCHET HOOK

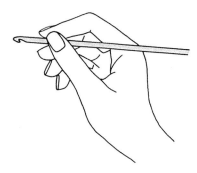

For most people the most flexible way to manipulate the hook is to hold it like a pencil. Alternatively, try holding it like a knife. Medium-size modern crochet hooks have a flattened portion on which the size is embossed, and this is the place to hold the hook in a light grip for maximum comfort and ease of movement.

MAKING A SLIP KNOT

There are several ways to make the first loop on the hook, but the most usual is the slip knot.

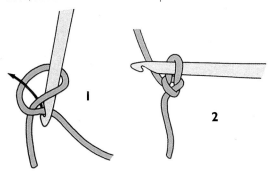

To make a slip knot, form a loop near the end of the yarn, with the end attached to the ball (the working end) lying on top. Insert the crochet hook into the loop from above, catch the working end and pull it through (1).

Pull on both ends of the yarn to make a knot, then pull the working end to close the knot up to the hook (2).

CONTROLLING THE YARN

The yarn is held in the hand not holding the hook, and is threaded through the fingers to maintain it at an even tension.

Try taking the yarn around the little finger, as shown in (1). Then hold the slip knot between thumb and first finger and extend the middle finger to support the yarn, as shown in (2). (Later, the thumb and first finger will hold the work.) If winding the yarn around the little finger puts too much brake on it, try letting it pass over three fingers then under the little finger and use the natural tendency to curl that finger to control the yarn. Another method is to hold the work between thumb and first finger and let the yarn pass over the first and second fingers, then under the third and over the fourth. Adopt any method that keeps the yarn fairly taut but moving smoothly.

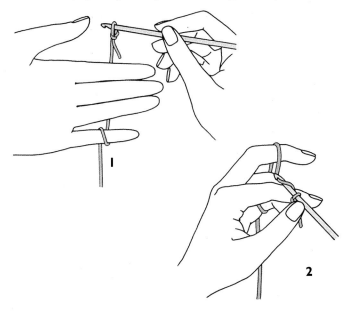

YARN ROUND HOOK
Abbreviation: yrh

Also sometimes called 'yarn over hook', this is the most basic movement in crochet. However, the phrase is slightly misleading, as it is actually the hook that goes round, then over the yarn.

Holding the slip knot between first finger and thumb (see Controlling the yarn, page 9), and keeping this hand still and the working yarn fairly taut, flex the hook hand so that the hook goes first under the yarn, from front to back, then over it. Catch the yarn in the hook (above) and, still holding the yarn taut, pull the hook back through the existing loop (1, right), thus forming a new loop. The more controlled the movement is, the more even the stitches will be.

STITCHES

The following are the basic stitches used in this book. Where they are combined to make other stitches, such as picots, they are explained in the instructions for the design.

All crochet stitches start and finish with a loop on the hook.

CHAIN
Abbreviation: ch

A series of loops – or in some cases only one loop – is referred to as 'chain'. Chain may be used as a foundation for stitches, to serve as a stitch at the beginning of a row or to create spaces within a fabric.

Make a slip knot to put the first loop on the hook. Take the yarn round the hook as described above, then gently pull the yarn through the loop on the hook (1) without tightening it too much.

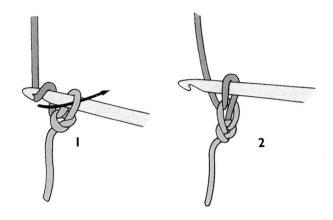

One chain has been completed (2). Repeat the two actions described above to make a continuous chain.

NOTE When counting chain do not include the slip knot or the loop on the crochet hook. If the chain is being used as the foundation for stitches worked in rows, it may be necessary to use a larger crochet hook for the chain to avoid producing a tight edge.

SLIP STITCH
Abbreviation: ss

This stitch has no height and is used mainly for joining, either to make chain into a ring or as an imperceptible join in a stitch pattern. It can also be used in shapings to carry the yarn along an edge and so avoid breaking off the yarn and re-joining it.

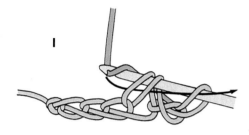

Insert the hook in the next stitch (or, in this case, the second chain from the hook), yarn round hook, pull the yarn through both the stitch and the loop on the hook (1). One slip stitch has been made.

NOTE The hook was inserted under the two strands of the V shape which forms the top of a stitch or the 'front' of a chain. *The hook is always inserted under the top two strands of all stitches and chain unless the instructions state otherwise.*

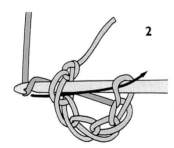

To join a length of chain into a ring with a slip stitch, insert the hook in the first chain, yarn round hook, pull the yarn through both the chain and the loop on the hook, then tighten to close up the ring (2). The slip stitch makes an invisible join and is not included in a stitch count.

DOUBLE CROCHET
Abbreviation: dc

The shortest of all the stitches used to make a fabric, double crochet is a firm stitch in its own right and a component of many other stitch patterns. Worked forward and back in rows, it makes ridges, each ridge comprising two rows.

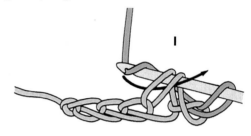

Insert the hook in the next stitch (or in this case, the second chain from the hook), yarn round hook, pull the yarn through the stitch only (1), making two loops on the hook.

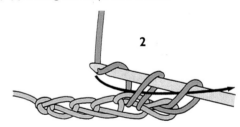

Yarn round hook, pull the yarn through both loops on the hook (2).

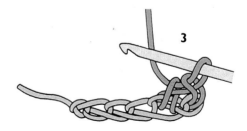

A double crochet has been made (3). This is the second stitch of the row, the first being the chain missed before making the stitch.

NOTE When double crochet is worked on a foundation chain two chain usually form the first stitch – one for the base of the stitch and one for the height. When double crochet is worked on the second and subsequent rows one chain forms the first stitch of each row. This chain is referred to as a stitch in a stitch count.

TREBLE
Abbreviation: tr

Taller than a double crochet, the treble is an even more versatile stitch, as it can be grouped, clustered or used on the surface of a crochet fabric. The extra height is the result of taking the yarn round the hook before inserting the hook in the next stitch.

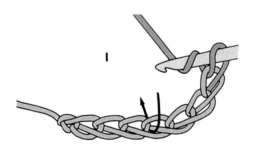

Yarn round hook and insert the hook in the next stitch (or in this case, the fourth chain from the hook) (1).

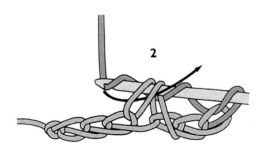

Yarn round hook and pull the yarn through the stitch only, making three loops on the hook (2).

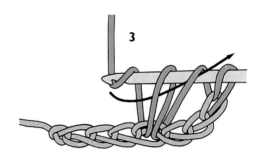

Yarn round hook and pull the yarn through the first two loops on the hook (3).

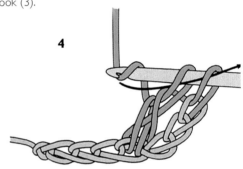

Yarn round hook and pull the yarn through the remaining two loops on the hook (4).

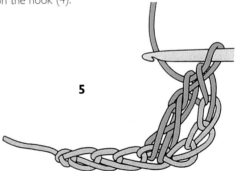

A treble has been made (5). This is the second stitch of the row, the first being the three chain missed before making the stitch.
NOTE For treble, three chain are required to form the first stitch of a row; this is included in a stitch count as one stitch.

DOUBLE TREBLE
Abbreviation: dtr

Taller stitches can be made by wrapping the yarn more times around the crochet hook. Double treble is made by taking the yarn round the hook twice before inserting the hook.

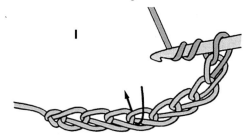

Yarn round hook twice and insert the hook in the next stitch (or in this case, the fifth chain from the hook) (1).

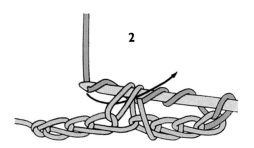

Yarn round hook and pull the yarn through the stitch only, making four loops on the hook (2).

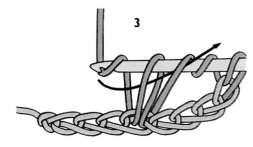

Yarn round hook and pull the yarn through the first two loops on the hook (3).

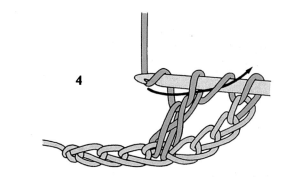

Yarn round hook and pull the yarn through the next two loops on the hook (4).

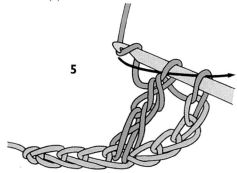

Yarn round hook and pull the yarn through the remaining two loops on the hook (5).

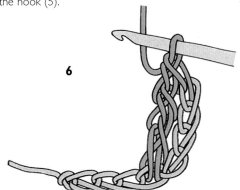

A double treble has now been made (6). This is the second stitch of the row, the first being the four chain missed before making the stitch.

TRIPLE TREBLE
Abbreviation: tr tr

As the name implies, triple treble is even taller than double treble. It's made by wrapping the yarn three times round the hook before inserting the hook in the next stitch (or the sixth chain from the hook). Then work as for double treble, noting that there are five loops on the hook in step 2 and repeat step 4 once before working step 5.

CRAB STITCH

Sometimes called corded edge stitch, this is simply double crochet worked from left to right instead of from right to left. It seems awkward at first and then becomes surprisingly easy. Worked on the right side of the fabric, usually with a hook one size smaller than used for the main part, each stitch makes a little knot.

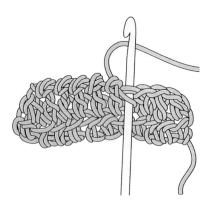

Insert the hook in the next stitch to the right, yarn round hook, draw through a loop, yarn round hook, draw through both loops on the hook.

POPCORN

A popcorn is a group of stitches gathered together at the top to form a firm, raised bobble. The popcorns used in this book are made with five treble stitches.

On a right-side row, make five trebles in one stitch. Take out the hook, leaving the loop. Insert the hook from front to back in the top of the first treble of the group, then into the loop.

Take the yarn round the hook and draw it through both loops on the hook to complete the popcorn.

WORKING AROUND A STITCH

Instead of working into the top of the next stitch in the row below, a stitch can be made around the stem of a stitch which is one, or even two, rows below. This makes the new stitch stand out in relief on the surface of the crochet.

This illustration shows the principle with a treble about to be worked around the stem of a treble in the row below, on the right side of the work. The stitch is made in the usual way but the hook is inserted from front to back, and then to the front again, around the stitch below.

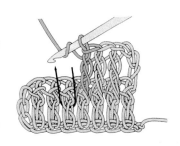

MAKING A FABRIC IN ROWS

By turning the work at the end of each row a flat fabric is made. As shown below, the first stitch of a row consists of chain. This and the fact that crochet stitches are not symmetrical can leave the beginner rather uncertain about how to begin and end rows to keep a straight edge and a regular stitch count. The principle, which is the same for all crochet worked in rows, is illustrated here with treble. Make 10 chain.

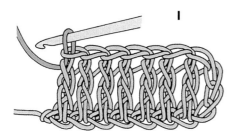

ROW 1 Miss 3 chain (to serve as first stitch), I treble in each of the remaining 7 chain. 8 stitches (1). Turn.

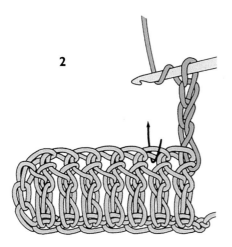

ROW 2 Make 3 chain (to serve as first stitch), I treble in the next stitch (i.e. not the stitch immediately below, or this will make an extra stitch – an increase) (2).

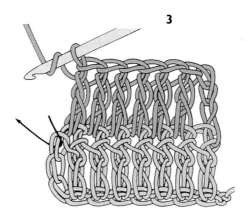

ROW 2 CONTINUED I treble in each of the remaining 5 treble, I treble in the top chain of the 3 chain. 8 stitches (3). Repeat row 2 throughout.

The illustrations show that both sides of a crochet fabric can look the same, so 'right' side and 'wrong' side are important only in relation to shapings or surface stitches.

FASTENING OFF

To fasten off at the end of the work, cut off the yarn, leaving an appropriate length, catch it with the crochet hook and pull it through the loop on the hook. Pull the end of yarn until the loop is lost and the yarn anchored.

FOLLOWING INSTRUCTIONS

The crochet designs in this collection are easy – in some cases very easy – to make; but even if you're not a beginner it's worth reading the following information to be sure you understand the way these instructions are set out.

TENSION

Working a preliminary tension piece is simply a means of ensuring that your work will be the intended size when it's finished. Tension is a given number of stitches to a given measurement. On a sample of the stitch to be used, measuring at least 12cm, 5in square, count the number of stitches across and the number of rows down as set out in 'Tension' in the instructions. Place pins outside these stitches and then measure the distance between the pins. If these measurements match those specified in the instructions, you can go ahead with that hook size. But if there's a discrepancy, experiment with a larger or smaller hook (larger if your measurement is smaller, and vice versa) until your tension matches that in the instructions.

BRACKETS

Both round and square brackets are used for specific functions in crochet instructions, as in knitting instructions.

Round brackets

Where a design is given in more than one size, round brackets are used to separate the larger sizes from the first, smallest, size, which stands in front of the brackets. Throughout a set of instructions figures relating to stitches, rows or measurements will be given in this sequence. Where one figure relates to all sizes only one figure is given.

Round brackets are also used to group instructions which are to be worked together – for example, a group of stitches to be worked into a single stitch. These round brackets have no figure in front of them and so can't be confused with those used for sizing.

Square brackets

Instructions that are to be repeated within a row, or a round in the case of circular items, are enclosed in square brackets. The number of repeats is given after the brackets.

ASTERISKS

A single asterisk, ★, is used in front of a section to be repeated within a row or round where the number of repeats isn't specified – for example, if it would be tedious to count a lot of small repeats.

Multiple asterisks, such as ★★ or ★★★, are used to indicate a larger section of instruction which is to be repeated, either up to the asterisks, after the asterisks or between sets of asterisks.

CHARTS AND SYMBOLS

Detailed instructions are given in this book and in some cases charts are given in addition to the row-by-row or round-by-round description. A chart can be followed without reference to the written instructions, if preferred, or the written instructions can be read in isolation from the accompanying chart. Many people will find it helpful to refer from one to the other, using the written explanation to get started or to familiarize themselves with a pattern repeat, then using the chart as a reminder of how many stitches there are in a pattern repeat, for example. It is much quicker to find your place in a chart than in lines of type. If you're not familiar with working from charts try a little cross-referencing in these simple designs and you will soon find that you are confident to tackle any chart. With minor variations, the symbols used in crochet charts are international and familiarity with them will enable you to sidestep foreign language barriers.

Symbols represent stitches, groups of stitches, increases, decreases, etc. and present a clear visual picture of how the elements of a design relate to each other. They also act as a useful reminder of what individual stitches consist of – for example, the horizontal line across the vertical upright of the symbol for a treble represents the single yarn-round-hook at the start of the stitch. In the same way, the double horizontal of a double treble represents the two yarn-round-hooks at the start of that stitch. The following is a list of the most commonly used symbols featured in this book.

○	chain	†	treble
•	slip stitch	‡	double treble
+	double crochet	‡	triple treble

Symbols for more unusual stitches specific to a particular design are shown with the chart for that design.

READING CHARTS

Charts for crochet worked in the round are read from the centre and from right to left – that is, in an anti-clockwise direction, exactly like the work itself. The rounds are coloured alternately in black and blue to make finding your place easier.

Charts for crochet worked in rows have alternate rows coloured in the same way. Where the rows are numbered, right-side rows numbered on the right of the chart are read from right to left; wrong-side rows numbered on the left are read from left to right. Most rounds and rows start with chain, so where there is no numbering the group of chain pinpoints the start and the round or row is then read from the chain, right to left on the right side and left to right on the wrong side.

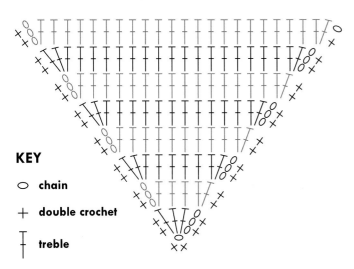

KEY

◯ **chain**

✛ **double crochet**

┬ **treble**

TECHNIQUES AND TIPS

The following information will be useful in working and completing some of the individual designs.

CHANGING COLOUR

The construction of crochet stitches makes it difficult to change neatly from one colour to another. This is less important at a row end which is going to be concealed in a seam than it is mid-row. The way to minimize any untidiness is to bring in the second colour before completing the last stitch in the first colour, whether colour-changing in a double crochet or treble fabric. In other words, work the last stitch in colour A until two loops of this stitch remain on the hook. Join colour B (1).

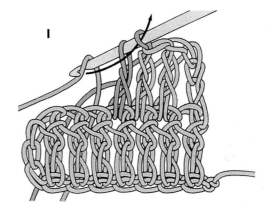

Use colour B to complete the stitch in the usual way and then continue with colour B (2).

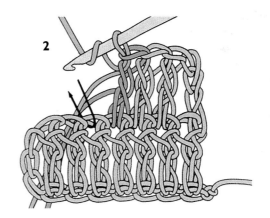

COLOUR PATTERNING

When working a two-colour motif or pattern in double crochet, make the colour change as above, i.e. using colour B to complete the last part of the last stitch in colour A, then carry A along the row until it's needed again. This is done by working each double crochet stitch around it. In other words, lay yarn A along the top of the next stitch, insert the hook in the stitch, take yarn B around the hook, pull it through the stitch, taking the hook over yarn A, catch yarn B and pull it through both loops on the hook. Continue in this way to the next colour change. This is also useful as a method of concealing ends without having to darn them in afterwards.

PRESSING

Note the recommendations on the yarn ball band as to the amount of heat to be applied and whether this should be applied dry or damp. All the designs in this collection are in yarns made from natural fibres and therefore were pressed damp. Before making up, each piece was pinned out to shape, right side downwards. Flat fabrics were pressed fairly firmly with a medium-hot iron over a damp muslin cloth. Textured fabrics were pressed in the same way but more gently and avoiding raised areas.

In order to pin out patchwork squares or shapes uniformly it's a good idea to draw the shape, with measurements taken from the instructions, on a piece of calico or similar fabric, using a waterproof felt pen. With this on the ironing board, every piece of crochet can be pinned out and pressed to an identical size and shape. This makes for much easier and neater joining up.

SEAMING AND JOINING

There are various ways to seam crochet. Normally, garment pieces are placed together with right sides facing and the edges oversewn or backstitched together. The seam will be less bulky if two strands of each adjacent stitch are worked into, rather than the whole stitch. Use a round-pointed wool needle to avoid splitting the yarn.

Patchwork, too, can be sewn in this way; but using double crochet to join pieces is speedier and gives an elastic seam. It can be done on the wrong side for an invisible join or it can be done on the right side for a decorative ridge.

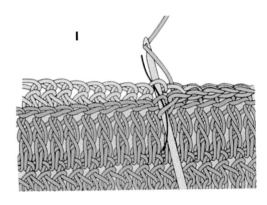

To join invisibly, place two patchwork pieces together with right sides together and insert the crochet hook in the inside single strand of the corresponding edge stitch of each piece (1), then work a double crochet through both stitches. Continue around the edge in this way.

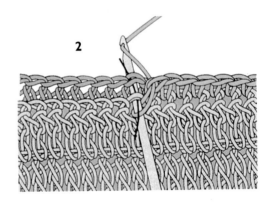

For a decorative ridge, place two patchwork pieces together with wrong sides together and work in double crochet under both strands of the corresponding edge stitch of each piece (2).

AFTERCARE

Crochet makes a very durable fabric and so, with appropriate care, garments and toys should have a long life. Hand-washing and drying flat are ideal but not always practical with children's things, so note the manufacturer's recommendations on the ball band.

TIPS

Here are a few suggestions to make your crochet easier or speedier or just more enjoyable.

❍ Holding a fine hook for long periods can put a strain on your hand so try pushing a cork onto the hook at the point where it's held, or even wrap sticking plaster around it to make things more comfortable.

❍ Using a rigid ruler to measure tension is preferable to using a tape measure. But if you use the latter avoid using the very end of it, which might be damaged. So, instead of measuring 1–10cm, measure 10–20cm.

❍ Taking the yarn from the middle of the ball, instead of from the outside will prevent it moving about as you work. This means gently pulling out the centre of the ball to locate the end.

❍ There are gadgets one can buy for marking particular stitches or rows, but the simplest and most convenient method is to use a short length of contrasting yarn. This is light, flexible and won't easily pull out.

❍ To mark a stitch simply lay the marker yarn across the work in front of the stitch, then bring the end of it back to the same side after the stitch has been made. Lightly knot the two ends if you think they need it.

❍ To mark a row take the marker yarn from front to back and vice versa between several stitches. This makes a row of what look like running stitches underneath the relevant row. To mark the end/beginning of rounds take the marker yarn from front to back, then back to front, between the last stitch of one round and the first stitch of the second round. This makes a row of 'running stitches' vertically up the work. All these markers are pulled out afterwards, leaving no trace.

ABBREVIATIONS

Many of the abbreviations used in crochet will be familiar to knitters. Beg, patt and tog, etc. appear very droll to those who don't follow crochet or knitting instructions but, far from being an esoteric language, they are a great help. They keep the instructions concise and therefore easier to understand and to find your place in.

beg	beginning
ch	chain
ch sp	chain space
cm	centimetres
cont	continu(e) (ing)
dc	double crochet
dec	decreas(e) (ing)
dtr	double treble
foll	following
in	inch(es)
inc	increas(e) (ing)
patt	pattern
rem	remain(ing)
rep	repeat
RS	right side
sp(s)	space(s)
ss	slip stitch
st(s)	stitch(es)
tog	together
tr	treble
trtr	triple treble
WS	wrong side
yrh	yarn round hook

SKY BLUE
AND CLOUD WHITE

There's no colour combination fresher than blue and white. It suggests

long summer days and holiday time, particularly when it's carried out in

crisp cotton. Nowadays, blue is no longer just for a boy and white

doesn't necessarily mean frills and femininity. Blue and white can be

used lavishly, together and separately.

Traditional smock

Fine baby yarn gives full, soft folds to this little smock. The horizontal rows and the vertical ribs make an easy-to-follow guide for the smocking, which decorates the yoke on the front and back. Button fastenings on each shoulder complete the simple style.

Materials

7 (8) 25g balls of Patons Baby Pure Wool 3-ply
2.00mm hook
6 small buttons

Size

To fit age 0–5 (5–10) months
actual size: chest 50 (58)cm, 19½ (22¾)in; length 35 (40)cm, 13¾ (15¾)in; sleeve 15 (18)cm, 6 (7)in

Tension

31 sts and 24 rows to 10cm, 4in over patt

Special Abbreviations (see page 19 for others)

dec 1dc = decrease 1dc: [insert hook in next st, yrh, draw loop through] twice, yrh, draw through all 3 loops on hook
dec 1tr = decrease 1tr: [yrh, insert hook in next st, yrh, draw loop through, yrh, draw through first 2 loops] twice, yrh, draw through all 3 loops on hook
dtr b = double treble in 2nd row below: taking hook to RS of work, miss dc in row below and work a dtr around the stem (see page 14) of tr in next row below
inc 1 = increase 1 st: work 2 tr in next st

Back

Make 115 (129) ch.
ROW 1 Miss 2 ch, ★ 1dc in next ch; rep from ★ to end. 114 (128) sts.
ROW 2 3 ch, ★1tr in next st; rep from ★, ending 1dc in top ch of 2 ch. Now patt thus:
ROW 3 (WS) 1ch, ★1dc in next st; rep from ★, ending 1dc in top ch of 3 ch.
ROW 4 3 ch, 1tr in each of next 3 sts, ★1 dtr b, 1tr in each of next 6 sts; rep from ★, ending 1 dtr b, 1tr in each of next 4 sts.

Rows 3 and 4 form patt.
Rep rows 3 and 4 until work measures 22 (25)cm, 8¾ (10)in, ending with a 3rd patt row.
DEC ROW (RS) Marking this row with contrasting yarn, work 3 ch, 1tr in each of next 3 sts, ★1 dtr b, 1tr in each of next 2 sts, dec 1tr, 1tr in each of next 2 sts; rep from ★, ending 1 dtr b, 1tr in each of next 4 sts. 99 (111) sts. ★★.
Working 5 tr instead of 6 tr between each pair of dtr b, work straight until work measures 25 (29) rows from marker, thus ending with a WS row.

NECK SHAPING

ROW 1 Patt 19 (25) sts, dec 1tr, turn.
Cont on these sts only for first side.
Patt 1 row.
Dec 1tr at neck edge on next row. 19 (25) sts.
Work 5 rows dc for button band. Fasten off.
NEXT ROW (RS) Miss centre 57 sts, rejoin yarn, dec 1tr, patt to end.
Complete to match first side.

Front

Work as Back to ★★.
Working 5 tr instead of 6 tr between each pair of dtr b, cont straight until work measures 21 (25) rows from marker, thus ending with a WS row.

NECK SHAPING

ROW 1 Patt 20 (26) sts, dec 1tr, turn.
Cont on these sts only for first side.
Dec 1tr at neck edge on foll 2 RS rows. 19 (25) sts.
Patt 2 rows straight, thus ending with a RS row.

BUTTONHOLE BAND

Work 2 rows dc.
NEXT ROW 1ch, 1dc in next st, 3 ch, miss 3 sts, [1dc in each of next 3 (6) sts, 3 ch, miss 3 sts] twice, 1dc in each of next 2 sts.

Working 1dc in each ch on first row, work 2 rows dc. Fasten off.

NEXT ROW (RS) Miss 55 sts, rejoin yarn, dec 1tr, patt to end.

Complete to match first side.

Sleeves

Make 52 (64) ch.

Work first row as first row of back. 51 (63) sts.

Work 2nd row as 2nd row of back.

Now patt thus:

ROW 3 (WS) 1ch, ★1dc in next st; rep from ★, ending 1dc in top ch of 3 ch.

ROW 4 3 ch, 1tr in each of next 3 sts, ★1 dtr b, 1tr in each of next 5 sts; rep from ★, ending 1 dtr b, 1tr in each of next 4 sts.

Rep rows 3 and 4 until work measures 9 (12) cm, 3½ (4¾) in, ending with a 3rd patt row.

Bringing inc sts into patt, inc 1 at each end of next 6 RS rows.

Patt 1 row. Fasten off.

CUFF

With RS facing, work into foundation ch: ★1dc, dec 1dc; rep from ★ to end. 34 (42) sts.

Work 5 rows dc. Fasten off.

Back Neckband

With RS facing, work 4 dc in end of button band, 1dc in each of next 3 row ends, [1dc, dec 1dc] 19 times across straight edge of neck, 1dc in each of next 3 row ends, 4 dc in end of button band.

Work 1 row dc. Fasten off.

Front Neckband

With RS facing, work 4 dc in end of buttonhole band, 2 dc in tr row ends and 1dc in dc row ends, [1dc, dec 1] 18 times, 1dc across straight edge of neck, 2 dc in tr row ends and 1dc in dc row ends and 4 dc in end of buttonhole band.

Work 1 row dc. Fasten off.

Smocking

No gathering is necessary, as the guidelines for the smocking are built into the crochet. The ribs made by the double trebles are pulled together with honeycomb smocking. This consists of pairs of stitches worked alternately in two rows. The stitches are positioned horizontally by being worked on double crochet rows only. Working two rows at a time with the yarn taken diagonally between them makes the smocking elastic. An additional single row of stitches has been added immediately below the neck to stabilize the gathers.

HOW TO SMOCK

Thread a wool needle with a single strand of yarn. With right side facing, starting at left of back neck, to left of first dtr rib and 2 dc rows down from neck, bring needle through to right side (1 in diagram right). Making st around next rib to right (2), bring needle out at 3, immediately below 1. Insert needle at 4 and bring it out beside rib on dc row below (5). Steps 6 and 7 correspond to steps 2 and 3. Step 8 is similar to step 4, but the needle is brought out in the first dc row at 9. In this way complete 2 rows of stitches across back neck. Repeat these 2 rows 3 times. Taking yarn horizontally from 1 pair of stitches to next, work one row of paired stitches across dc row immediately below neck. Smock panel below front neck the same.

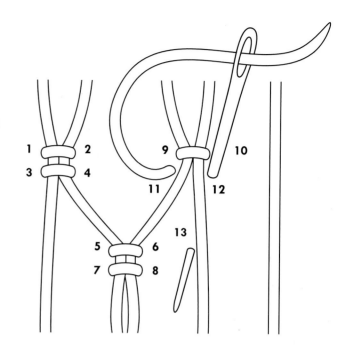

To Complete

Tack the buttonhole band over the button band on each shoulder. Centre the top edge of a sleeve on each buttonhole band and sew on the sleeves. Join side and sleeve seams. Sew on buttons.

Idea: add colour and bullion knot roses to the smocking.

Use a contrasting colour of 3-strand embroidery wool or stranded embroidery cotton for the smocking and decoration. To make a bullion knot wind the thread around the needle as shown (left), then pull the needle and thread through the wraps. Re-insert the needle at the original insertion point. Work 3 or 4 bullion knots close together to form a rose.

Heirloom quilt

A Victorian-style white cotton quilt is unashamedly nostalgic. This one is composed of squares, each one with a star motif, and finished with a lacy edging. The stars are worked in 'popcorns', which give a rich, embossed texture.

Materials

15 50g balls Rowan 4-ply Cotton in white
2.00mm hook

Size

One square measures approximately 16cm, 6¼in
The cover measures approximately 80cm x 112cm, 31½in x 44in, excluding edging

Tension

18 sts and 12 rows to 10cm, 4in over tr

Special Abbreviations (see page 19 for others)

p = picot: 3 ch, 1dc in first ch
pc = popcorn: work 5 tr in one st, take out hook leaving loop, insert hook from front to back in top of first tr then into loop, yrh, draw yarn through (see illustration on page 14)

Square

Make 5 ch, ss into first ch to form a ring.
Work in rounds with RS facing:
ROUND 1 3 ch, working into ring plus yarn end, make 15 tr in ring, join with ss to top ch of 3 ch.
ROUND 2 4 ch, 1tr in st below, ★ 2 tr in next st, 1pc in next st, 2 tr in

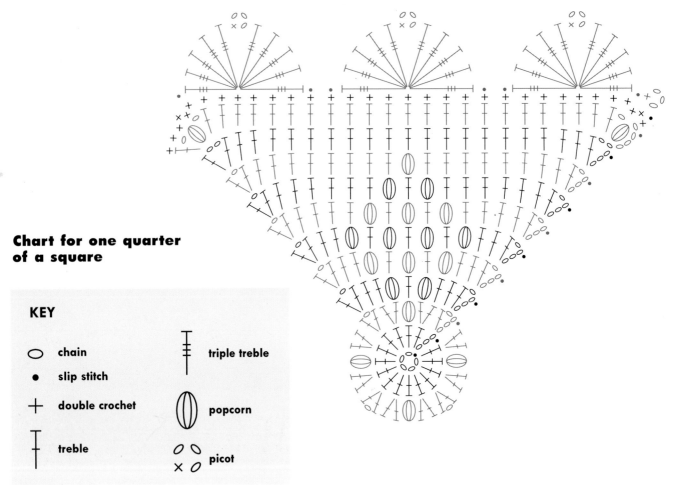

Chart for one quarter of a square

KEY

⬯	chain	⟊	triple treble
•	slip stitch	⬮	popcorn
+	double crochet		
⟙	treble	⬯⬯ / × ⬯	picot

next st, (1tr, 1ch, 1tr) in next st; rep from ★ twice, 2 tr in next st, 1pc in next st, 2 tr in next st, ss to 3rd of 4 ch.

ROUND 3 4 ch, 1tr in ch sp below, ★ 1tr in each of next 2 sts, 1pc in next st, 1tr in next st, 1pc in next st, 1tr in each of next 2 sts, (1tr, 1ch, 1tr) in ch sp; rep from ★ twice, 1tr in each of next 2 sts, 1pc in next st, 1tr in next st, 1pc in next st, 1tr in each of next 2 sts, ss to 3rd of 4 ch.

ROUND 4 4 ch, 1tr in ch sp below, ★ 1tr in each of next 2 sts, [1pc in next st, 1tr in next st] twice, 1pc in next st, 1tr in each of next 2 sts, (1tr, 1ch, 1tr) in ch sp; rep from ★, ending 1tr in each of next 2 sts, ss to 3rd of 4 ch.

ROUND 5 4 ch, 1tr in ch sp below, ★ 1tr in each of next 2 sts, [1pc in

next st, 1tr in next st] 3 times, 1pc in next st, 1tr in each of next 2 sts, (1tr, 1ch, 1tr) in ch sp; rep from ★, ending 1tr in each of next 2 sts, ss to 3rd of 4 ch.

ROUND 6 4 ch, 1tr in ch sp below, ★ 1tr in each of next 4 sts, [1pc in next st, 1tr in next st] twice, 1pc in next st, 1tr in each of next 4 sts, (1tr, 1ch, 1tr) in ch sp; rep from ★, ending 1tr in each of next 4 sts, ss to 3rd of 4 ch.

ROUND 7 4 ch, 1tr in ch sp below, ★ 1tr in each of next 6 sts, 1pc in next st, 1tr in next st, 1pc in next st, 1tr in each of next 6 sts, (1tr, 1ch, 1tr) in ch sp; rep from ★, ending 1tr in each of next 6 sts, ss to 3rd of 4 ch.

ROUND 8 4 ch, 1tr in ch sp below, ★ 1tr in each of next 8 sts, 1pc in next st, 1tr in each of next 8 sts, (1tr, 1ch, 1tr) in ch sp; rep from ★, ending 1tr in each of next 8 sts, ss to 3rd of 4 ch.

ROUND 9 5 ch, 1tr in ch sp below, ★ 1tr in each of next 19 sts, (1tr, 2 ch, 1tr) in ch sp; rep from ★, ending 1tr in each of next 19 sts, ss to 3rd of 5 ch.

ROUND 10 4 ch, (1pc, 1ch, 1tr) in ch sp below, ★ 1tr in each of next 21 sts, (1tr, 1ch, 1pc, 1ch, 1tr) in ch sp; rep from ★, ending 1tr in each of next 21 sts, ss to 3rd of 4 ch. Fasten off. Make 35 squares.

To Complete

Taking care not to flatten the popcorns, pin out squares and press (see page 18). With right sides together, join 35 squares with dc on wrong side (see page 18) into a rectangle of 5 squares × 7 squares.

Edging

With RS facing, join yarn in one corner and work:

ROUND 1 3 dc in pc, 1dc in ch sp, 1dc in each of next 23 tr, 1dc in ch sp, 1dc in pc; ★1dc in pc, 1dc in ch sp, 1dc in each of next 23 tr, 1dc in ch sp, 1dc in pc; rep from ★, working 3 dc in each corner pc and ending 1dc in ch sp, ss to first dc.

ROUND 2 1p in centre dc of 3 corner dc, ★ ss in next dc, miss 3 dc, (5 trtr, 1p, 5 trtr) in next dc, miss 3 dc, ss in next dc; rep from ★, making 3 scallops along each square, to next corner, 1p in centre dc of 3 corner dc. Work each edge the same, ending with ss in first st. Fasten off.

Idea: use the same 'popcorns' around the centre of a daisy.

Materials

Rowan 4-ply Cotton in blue
2.00mm hook

Special Abbreviations (see page 19 for others)

cl = cluster: ★ yrh twice, insert hook, draw yarn through, (yrh, draw yarn through first 2 loops on hook) twice, rep from ★ twice, yrh, draw yarn through all 4 loops on hook

pc = popcorn: work 5 tr in 1 st, take out hook leaving loop, insert hook from front to back in top of first tr then into loop, yrh, draw yarn through (illustration on page 14)

To Make

Worked in rounds with RS facing.
Make 8 ch. Ss into first ch to form a ring.

ROUND 1 1ch, 15 dc in ring, ss first ch.

ROUND 2 4 ch, 1pc in next dc, 1ch, ★1tr in next dc, 1ch, 1pc in next dc, 1ch; rep from ★ 6 times, ss to 3rd of 4 ch.

ROUND 3 4 ch, (1cl, 4 ch, 1dc) in ch below, ★(1dc, 4 ch, 1cl, 4 ch, 1dc) in next tr; rep from ★ 6 times, ss to ch below first 4 ch. Fasten off.

Blues blanket

Every shade of blue has been used in this patchwork blanket, designed specially for the baby who wears denim. Working into the back of each stitch gives it a deep, furrowed texture and, to minimize sewing up, it's made from strips worked in stripes to look like squares, or blocks.

Materials

Double Knitting yarn in many shades of blue, the first 7 designated A, B, C, D, E, F and G
3.50mm hook

Tension

Approximately 20 sts and 26 rows to 10cm, 4in over dc

Size

Each block measures approximately 11cm, 4½in square once the strips are joined, so the finished blanket can be any multiple of 11cm, 4½in. This one is made up of 6 strips, each 8 blocks long, which makes its size approximately 66cm x 88cm, 26in x 34½in excluding the edging

Abbreviations (see page 19)

Plain Block

Using A, make 25 ch.
ROW 1 Miss 2 ch, 1dc in each ch to end. 24 sts.
ROW 2 1ch, ★ working into the back strand only of the 2 strands which form the top of the st, work 1dc in next dc; rep from ★, ending 1dc in ch.
Rep row 2 28 times, making a total of 30 rows (15 ridges on RS).
Do not fasten off unless this is the last block of the strip.

Block with Narrow Stripes

Using B, make 25 ch and work row 1 as for plain block only if this is the first block of a strip, counting this row as the first row of the first stripe. Otherwise:

ROWS 1 AND 2 Using B, 1ch, ★ working into the back strand as before, 1dc in next st; rep from ★, ending 1dc in 1ch.

ROWS 3 AND 4 Using C, as rows 1 and 2.

Rep rows 1–4 6 times, then work rows 1 and 2 again, making a total of 30 rows.

Do not fasten off unless this is the last block of the strip.

Block with Medium Stripes

Using D, make 25 ch and work row 1 as for plain block only if this is the first block of a strip, counting this row as the first row of the first stripe. Otherwise:

ROWS 1 AND 2 Using D, 1ch, ★ working into the back strand as before, 1dc in next dc; rep from ★, ending 1dc in ch.

ROWS 3 AND 4 Using E, as rows 1 and 2.

ROWS 5 AND 6 Using D, as rows 1 and 2.

Rep rows 1–6 4 times, making a total of 30 rows.

Do not fasten off unless this is the last block of the strip.

Block with Wide Stripes

Using F, make 25 ch and work row 1 as for plain block only if this is the first block of a strip, counting this row as the first row of the first stripe. Otherwise:

ROWS 1, 2, 3 AND 4 Using F, 1ch, ★ working into the back strand as before, 1dc in next dc; rep from ★, ending 1dc in 1ch.

ROWS 5 AND 6 Using G, as rows 1 and 2.

ROWS 7, 8, 9 AND 10 Using F, as rows 1, 2, 3 and 4.

Rep rows 1–10 twice more, making a total of 30 rows.

Do not fasten off unless this is the last block of the strip.

Design

Mix plain and striped blocks as much as you like. Putting tonal contrasts together has more impact than putting similar tones together. Vary the medium and wide striped blocks by putting pale stripes on dark and vice versa.

To Complete

On the wrong side and matching rows carefully, backstitch the strips together. Press lightly (see page 18).

Edging

With RS facing, join yarn in one corner and, working 3 dc in each corner, work a round of dc, followed by a second round the same. Fasten off.

Idea: use the same technique to make a cushion.

Materials

Double Knitting yarn in shades of yellow and orange
Cushion pad 35cm, 14in square
3.50mm hook

To Make

Work 6 strips of 3 blocks each, as for blues blanket. Join 3 strips for the front and 3 strips for the back of the cushion. Join these, enclosing the cushion pad.

Matelot jacket

A much-loved classic is the collarless jacket with drop shoulders and crisp navy-on-white stripes. It's sturdier than a knitted cardigan and has quite a nautical air.

Materials

3 100g balls of Patons Cotton 4-ply: 2 balls in white (A) and 1 ball in navy (B)
2.00mm and 3.00mm hooks
5 buttons

Size

To fit age 3 months (6 months, 12 months, 18 months, 2 years) actual size: chest 60 (63, 67, 69, 71) cm, 23½ (24¾, 26¼, 27¼, 28) in; length 22 (24, 26, 28, 30) cm, 8¾ (9½, 10¼, 11, 11¾) in; sleeve 18 (21, 23, 26, 28) cm, 7 (8¼, 9, 10¼, 11) in, with cuff not turned back

Tension

22 sts and 28 rows to 10cm, 4in over dc using 3.00mm hook

Special Abbreviations (see page 19 for others)

dec 1 = decrease 1 st: [insert hook in next st, yrh, draw loop through] twice, yrh, draw through all 3 loops on hook
inc 1 = increase 1 st: work 2 dc in next st

Back

Using 3.00mm hook and A, make 67 (71, 75, 77, 79) ch.
ROW 1 (RS) Miss 2 ch, ★1dc in next ch; rep from ★ to end. 66 (70, 74, 76, 78) sts.
ROW 2 1ch, ★1dc in next dc; rep from ★, ending 1dc in top ch of 2 ch.
ROW 3 1ch, ★1dc in next dc; rep from ★, ending 1dc in 1ch.
Rep row 3 once.
With B, rep row 3 twice.
Carrying yarn not in use up side edge, cont straight working 4 rows A and 2 rows B (6-row stripe patt), until a total of 58 (64, 70, 76, 82) rows has been completed.
NECK SHAPING
ROW 1 (RS) Patt 22 (23, 25, 25, 26) sts, dec 1 st, work 1dc, turn.

Cont on these sts only for first side.
Keeping patt correct, dec 1 st, one st in from neck edge, on next 3 rows.
Fasten off.
NEXT ROW (RS) Miss centre 16 (18, 18, 20, 20) sts, rejoin yarn, 1ch, dec 1 st, patt to end.
Complete to match first side.

Left Front

Using 3.00mm hook and A, make 33 (35, 37, 38, 39) ch.

ROW 1 (RS) As row 1 of back. 32 (34, 36, 37, 38) sts.

Cont as back from row 2 until a total of 50 (54, 60, 64, 70) rows has been completed. ★★.

NECK SHAPING

ROW 1 (RS) Patt 24 (25, 27, 27, 28) sts, dec 1 st, work 1dc, turn.

Cont on these sts only.

Keeping patt correct, dec 1 st, one st in from neck edge, on next 5 rows. 21 (22, 24, 24, 25) sts.

Patt 6 (8, 8, 10, 10) rows straight.

Fasten off.

Right Front

Work as left front to ★★.

Fasten off.

NECK SHAPING

ROW 1 (RS) Miss first 5 (6, 6, 7, 7) sts, rejoin yarn, 1ch, dec 1 st, patt to end.

Complete to match left front.

Sleeves

Using 3.00mm hook and A, make 33 (36, 38, 39, 41) ch.

ROW 1 (RS) As first row of back. 32 (35, 37, 38, 40) sts.

Patt 3 (3, 3, 1, 1) rows as for beg of back.

FIRST INC ROW 1ch, inc 1, patt to last 2 sts, inc 1, 1dc.

Cont to inc thus on every foll 6th row until there are 48 (53, 57, 62, 66) sts.

Patt 3 (5, 5, 3, 3) rows straight, making a total of 50 (58, 64, 72, 78) rows.

Fasten off.

Front and Neckband

Join shoulder seams.

Using 2.00mm hook and A, and with RS facing, work 1dc in each row end up right front, 3 dc in top corner st, 1dc in each st and row end around back neck, 3 dc in top corner st of left front, 1dc in each row end down left front.

ROW 2 1ch, ★1dc in next st; rep from ★ to end.

ROW 3 (BUTTONHOLE ROW) 1ch, 1dc in each of next 2 (2, 4, 4, 6) sts, 3 ch, miss 3 sts, [1dc in each of next 8 (9, 10, 11, 12) sts, 3 ch, miss 3 sts] 4 times, working 2 dc in both top corners, work in dc to end.

ROW 4 As row 2.

ROW 5 Working 3 dc in both top corners, work in dc to end.

Fasten off.

To Complete

Press. Matching stripes at underarm, sew on sleeves. Join side and sleeve seams, reversing seams at cuffs for turn-back. Sew on buttons.

Idea: if you prefer, reverse the colours to white on navy and add brass buttons.

Materials

Patons Cotton 4-ply: 2 balls navy (A) and 1 ball white (B)

To Make

Work as previous version of Matelot Jacket.

Classic sun hat

This style of cotton hat with a deep crown and rolled brim is a long-time children's favourite.

Materials

1 (1, 2) 100g balls of Patons Cotton 4-ply in white
2.50mm hook

Size

To fit age 1 (2, 3) years

Tension

24 sts and 30 rows to 10cm, 4in over dc

Abbreviations (see page 19)

Crown

Make 4 ch, ss into first ch to form a ring.
Work in rounds with RS facing.
ROUND 1 1ch, 7 dc in ring, ss in ch. 8 sts.
The rounds are now worked continuously, so mark the beginning of each round with contrasting yarn (see page 19).

ROUND 2 [1 dc in next st, 2 dc in next st] 4 times. 12 sts.
ROUND 3 [1 dc in next st, 2 dc in next st] 6 times. 18 sts.
ROUND 4 [1 dc in each of next 2 sts, 2 dc in next st] 6 times. 24 sts.
ROUND 5 [1 dc in each of next 3 sts, 2 dc in next st] 6 times. 30 sts.
ROUND 6 [1 dc in each of next 4 sts, 2 dc in next st] 6 times. 36 sts.
Cont to inc 6 sts each round, working 1 st more before each inc on each round, until there are 90 (96, 102) sts, then on alternate rounds until there are 114 (120, 126) sts ★★.
Work straight for 6 (7, 8)cm, 2¼ (2¾, 3¼)in.

Shape Brim

INC ROUND [1 dc in each of next 2 sts, 2 dc in next st] to end.
152 (160, 168) sts.
Work 10 (12, 14) rounds straight.
DEC ROUND ★1 dc in each of next 6 sts, [insert hook in next st and draw loop through] twice, yrh and draw through all 3 loops; rep from ★ to end. 133 (140, 147) sts.
Work 1 round, ss in next st. Fasten off.

Idea: leave off the brim and simply roll the lower edge for an alternative style.

Materials

1 (1, 2) 100g balls Patons Cotton 4-ply in blue
2.50mm hook

To Make

Work as Classic Sun Hat to ★★.
Work straight for 14 (15, 16)cm, 5½ (6, 6¼)in, ss in next st.
Fasten off.
Fold up edge.

Small sandals

First-size cotton sandals are completely frivolous, but they could look very chic at the seaside.

Materials

1 50g ball of Rowan 4-ply cotton in white
1.50mm and 2.00mm hooks
2 small buttons

Size

To fit age birth–3 months. Actual length approximately 8cm, 3¼in

Tension

25 sts and 30 rows to 10cm, 4in over dc using 2.00mm hook

Abbreviations (see page 19)

To Make

SOLE Worked around a straight ch, RS facing. Mark beg of each round with contrasting yarn (see page 19).
Using 2.00mm hook, make 13 ch.
ROUND 1 Miss 2 ch, 1 dc in each of next 11 ch, 2 ch, swivel work, [1 dc in rem strand of next ch] 12 times, 2 ch.
ROUND 2 [1 dc in each of next 12 sts, 3 dc in 2 ch sp at end] twice.
ROUND 3 [1 dc in each of next 12 sts, 2 dc in each of 3 end sts] twice.
ROUND 4 [1 dc in each of next 12 sts, 1 dc in each of 6 end sts] twice.

ROUND 5 [1 dc in each of next 12 sts, 2 dc in each of 6 end sts] twice.
ROUND 6 [1 dc in each of next 12 sts, 1 dc in each of 12 end sts] twice.
ROW 7 1 dc in each of next 28 sts, ss in next st, turn.
ROW 8 1 dc in each of next 17 sts, ss in next st. Fasten off.
Make another sole to match.

LEFT HEEL
Make 10 ch.
ROW 1 Miss 2 ch, ★1 dc in next ch; rep from ★ to end. 9 sts.
ROW 2 1 ch, ★1 dc in next st; rep from ★ to end. ★★.
Rep row 2 22 times.

ANKLE STRAP
Make 19 ch, miss 2 ch, 1 dc in each of rem 17 ch, 1 dc in each of next 9 sts. 27 sts.
NEXT ROW 1 ch, 1 dc in each of next 21 sts, 3 ch, miss 3 sts, 1 dc in each of rem 2 sts.
NEXT ROW 1 ch, ★1 dc in next st; rep from ★ to end. Fasten off.

RIGHT HEEL
As left heel.

TOE STRAP
Make 21 ch.
ROW 1 Miss 2 ch, 1 dc in each of rem 19 ch. 20 sts.
ROWS 2 AND 3 1 ch, 1 dc in each of next 19 sts. Fasten off.

Idea: alter the colour and trim for a change of mood.

Materials

1 ball of Rowan 4-ply Cotton in blue
2.00mm and 1.50mm hooks
2 small buttons

To Make

Work as for Small sandals, but work row of crab stitch (dc worked from left to right – see page 14) around sole only.

CENTRE STRAP

Make 24 ch.

ROW 1 Miss 2 ch, 1dc in next ch, 4 ch, miss 4 ch, 1dc in each of next 5 ch, 4 ch, miss 4 ch, 1dc in each of rem 8 ch.

ROW 2 1 ch, 1dc in each of next 22 sts.

ROW 3 1 ch, 1dc in next st, 4 ch, miss 4 sts, 1dc in each of next 5 sts, 4 ch, miss 4 sts, 1dc in each of rem 8 sts. Fasten off.

To Complete

Without stretching heel, fit heel around narrow end of sole. Using running stitch and working on RS, stitch left heel to one sole. Stitch right heel to second sole, strap to opposite side. Stitch solid end of centre strap to centre front of sole. Using 1.50mm hook, work a row of crab stitch (see page 14) along both long edges of toe strap and around centre strap. Thread toe strap through slots in middle of centre strap and stitch each end of toe strap to sole. Using 1.50mm hook and with RS facing, work a row of crab stitch around sole, taking hook through both layers where heel and toe strap are attached to sole. Work a row of crab stitch around rem edges of heel and ankle strap. Thread ankle strap through centre strap slots. Sew on buttons.

CHALKY PASTELS

If you exclude candy pink and all the sugary confectionery colours, pastels can be very sophisticated. From soft, cloudy lilac to sharp eau de nil, from pale vanilla to duck egg blue, these colours look wonderful in a modern nursery. Used singly or together, they flatter most colourings and aren't just for little girls, either.

Cross your heart

Heart-shaped motifs set in squares make a glorious pastel-coloured blanket or cot cover.

Materials

Double Knitting yarn in pastel colours (each square is made up of three colours or tones, A, B and C)
3.00mm and 3.50mm hooks

Size

Each square measures approximately 10cm, 4in

Tension

Approximately 20 sts and 26 rows to 10cm, 4in over dc

Abbreviations (see page 19)

Heart Square

Using 3.50mm hook and A, make 7 ch, ss into first ch to make a ring. Work in rounds with RS facing.

ROUND 1 3ch, 19 tr in ring, ss to top ch of 3 ch. 20 sts.

ROUND 2 1ch, 2 dc in next st, [1tr in next st, 2 tr in next st] 8 times, 1tr in next st, 2 dc in next st, ss to ch.

ROUND 3 1ch, 2 dc in next st, 1tr in next st, 2 tr in each of next 4 sts, 1tr in next st, 1dc in each of next 5 sts, 2 tr in each of next 2 sts, (1tr, 1dtr, 1tr) in next st, 2 tr in each of next 2 sts, 1dc in each of next 5 sts, 1tr in next st, 2 tr in each of next 4 sts, 1tr in next st, 2 dc in next st, ss to ch. Fasten off A.

ROUND 4 Using B and starting at base of heart, (1ch, 1dc) in dtr, 1dc in each of next 22 sts, 1dc in ch 2 rounds below, 1dc in each of next 22 sts, 1dc in dtr, ss to ch.

ROUND 5 1ch, 1dc in each of next 2 sts, 1tr in each of next 2 sts, 1dtr in next st, (1trtr, 1ch, 1trtr) in next st, 1dtr in next st, 1tr in each of next 2 sts, 1dc in each of next 6 sts, 1tr in each of next 2 sts, (1dtr, 1ch, 1dtr) in next st, 1tr in next st, 1dc in each of next 3 sts, 1tr in

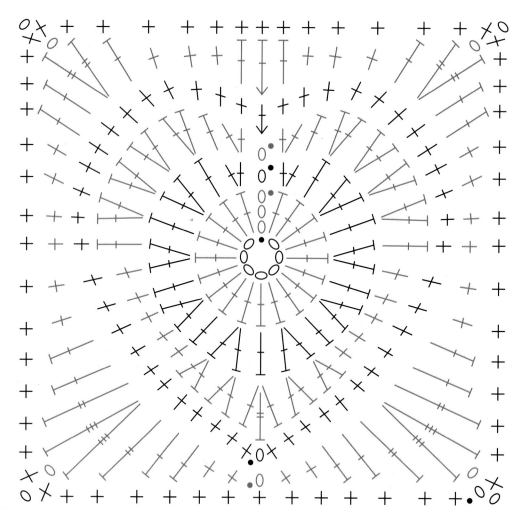

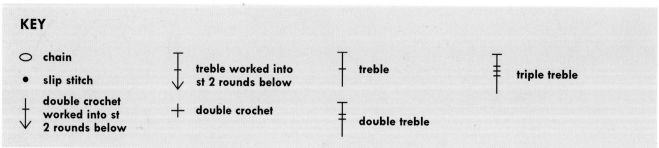

KEY

○ chain

● slip stitch

double crochet worked into st 2 rounds below

treble worked into st 2 rounds below

+ double crochet

treble

double treble

triple treble

next st, 1tr in centre st 2 rounds below, 1tr in next st, 1dc in each of next 3 sts, 1tr in next st, (1trtr, 1ch, 1trtr) in next st, 1tr in each of next 2 sts, 1dc in each of next 6 sts, 1tr in each of next 2 sts, 1dtr in next st, (1dtr, 1ch, 1dtr) in next st, 1dtr in next st, 1tr in each of next 2 sts, 1dc in next 2 sts, ss to ch. Fasten off B.

ROUND 6 Using C and starting at one corner, (2 ch, 1dc) in ch sp, ★1dc in each of next 13 sts, (1dc, 1ch, 1dc) in ch sp; rep from ★ 3 times, ending ss in first ch. Fasten off.

To Complete

Square up and press motifs (see page 18). Join by placing squares wrong sides together and joining with dc (see page 18).

Edging

Using 3.00mm hook and with RS facing, work a row of crab stitch (dc worked from left to right – see page 14). Work 2 sts into each corner.

Idea: two heart motifs can be joined together to make a pretty lavender sachet.

Materials

Double Knitting yarn in two pastel colours, A and B
2.50mm and 3.00mm hooks
Piece of toning fabric at least 10cm x 20cm, 4in x 8in
40cm, ½yd narrow ribbon
Lavender
Water-soluble fabric marker
Sewing needle and thread

Size

Approximately 7.5cm x 7.5cm, 3in x 3in

To Make

Using 3.00mm hook and A, work as Heart Square to the end of round 3. Fasten off. Make another motif in the same way.

Inner Cover

Using a crochet heart shape as a template, draw two heart shapes on the fabric with the water-soluble marker, adding 1cm, ⅜in seam allowance. Cut out. Stitch the two hearts together along the drawn line, leaving a small opening. Trim seam to approximately 3mm, ⅛in. Turn the bag right side out and fill with lavender, then slipstitch the gap to close it.

To Complete

Join the two crochet hearts by holding them with wrong sides together and, using 2.50mm hook and B, work round 4 of heart square through both layers of crochet (see page 18). Before completing the round, insert the fabric bag. Make a loop in the middle of the ribbon and use a crochet hook to pull the loop through the centre top of heart from front to back. Tie the ends in a bow and trim as required.

Sweetheart jacket

A Peter Pan collar is the special feature of this little jacket with curved fronts. It also has mother-of-pearl buttons and a narrow lacy edging.

Materials

4 (5) 50g balls of Jaeger Baby Merino 4-ply in lilac
2.50mm and 3.00mm hooks
3 buttons

Size

To fit age 18 months (2 years)
Actual size: chest 61 (71)cm, 24 (28)in; length 25 (28)cm, 10 (11)in excluding edging; sleeve 16 (19)cm, 6¼ (7½)in excluding edging

Tension

24 sts and 13½ rows to 10cm, 4in over tr using 3.00mm hook

Special Abbreviations (see page 19 for others)

dec 1 = decrease 1 st: [yrh, insert hook in next st, yrh, draw through loop, yrh, draw through first 2 loops on hook] twice, yrh, draw through all 3 loops on hook;
inc 1 – increase 1 st: work 2 tr in next st

Back

Using 3.00mm hook, make 75 (87) ch.
ROW 1 (RS) Miss 3 ch, ★1tr in next ch; rep from ★ to end. 73 (85) sts.
ROW 2 3 ch, ★1tr in next st; rep from ★, ending 1tr in top ch of 3 ch.
Rep row 2 until a total of 32 (36) rows has been completed.
NECK SHAPING
ROW 1 (RS) 3 ch, 1tr in each of next 22 (26) sts, [dec 1] twice, 1dtr in next st, turn.
Cont on these sts only for first side.
ROW 2 4 ch, [dec 1] twice, ★1tr in next st; rep from ★ to end. 24 (28) sts. Fasten off.
NEXT ROW (RS) Miss centre 17 (21) sts, rejoin yarn, 4 ch in first st, [dec 1] twice, ★1tr in next st; rep from ★, ending 1tr in top ch of 3 ch.

NEXT ROW 3 ch, 1tr in each of next 20 (24) sts, [dec 1] twice, 1dtr in last st. 24 (28) sts.
Fasten off.

Left Front

Using 3.00mm hook, make 32 (38) ch.
ROW 1 (RS) Miss 3 ch, 1tr in each of next 26 (32) ch, [inc 1] twice, 1dtr in last ch. 32 (38) sts.
ROW 2 4 ch, [inc 1] twice, ★1tr in next st; rep from ★, ending 1tr in top ch of 3 ch.
ROW 3 3 ch, 1tr in each of next 30 (36) sts, [inc 1] twice, 1dtr in last st.
Rep last 2 rows once. 40 (46) sts.
Work straight until a total of 28 (32) rows has been completed.
NECK SHAPING
ROW 1 (RS) 3 ch, 1tr in each of next 26 (30) sts, [dec 1] twice, 1dtr in last st; turn. 30 (34) sts.
Cont on these sts only.
ROW 2 4 ch, [dec 1] twice, ★1tr in next st; rep from ★, ending 1tr in top ch of 3 ch.
ROW 3 Work to last 5 sts, [dec 1] twice, 1dtr.
ROW 4 As row 2. 24 (28) sts.
Work 2 rows straight. Fasten off.

Right Front

Using 3.00mm hook, make 33 (39) ch.
ROW 1 (RS) Miss 4 ch, [inc 1] twice, ★1tr in next ch; rep from ★ to end. 32 (38) sts.
ROW 2 3 ch, 1tr in each of next 28 (34) sts, [inc 1] twice, 1dtr in top ch of 4 ch.
ROW 3 4 ch, [inc 1] twice, ★1tr in next st; rep from ★, ending 1tr in top ch of 3 ch.
Rep last 2 rows once. 40 (46) sts.

Work straight until a total of 10 (14) rows has been completed.

FIRST BUTTONHOLE ROW (RS) 3 ch, 1tr in each of next 2 sts, 1ch, miss 1tr, ★1tr in next st; rep from ★, ending 1tr in top ch of 4 ch. Make 2 more buttonholes in this way, with 7 rows between each. Work 1 row after last buttonhole. Fasten off.

NECK SHAPING

NEXT ROW (RS) Miss 8 (10) sts, rejoin yarn, 4 ch in this st, [dec 1] twice, ★1tr in next st; rep from ★, ending 1tr in top ch of 4 ch. Complete to match left front.

Sleeves

Using 3.00mm hook, make 37 (43) ch.

ROW 1 (RS) As first row of back. 35 (41) sts.

ROW 2 3 ch, inc 1, ★1tr in next st; rep from ★ to last 2 sts, inc 1, 1tr in top ch of 3 ch. 37 (43) sts.

ROW 3 3 ch, ★1tr in next st; rep from ★, ending 1tr in top ch of 3 ch. Rep these 2 rows until there are 57 (67) sts, a total of 22 (26) rows. Fasten off.

Collar

Using 3.00mm hook, make 65 (73) ch.

ROW 1 (RS) As first row of back. 63 (71) sts.

ROW 1 Work 1 (5) sts, inc 1, [1tr in each of next 5 sts, inc 1] 10

times, work 1 (5) sts. 74 (82) sts.

Work 1 row.

NEXT ROW 3 ch, inc 1, ★1tr in next st; rep from ★ to last 2 sts, inc 1, 1tr in last st.

Rep last 2 rows once. 78 (86) sts.

Work 1 row.

FIRST DEC ROW 4 ch, [dec 1] twice, ★1tr in next st; rep from ★ to last 5 sts, [dec 1] twice, 1dtr in top ch of 4 ch.

Rep this row twice. 66 (74) sts.

Fasten off.

To Complete

Press. Join shoulder seams. At neck, place markers 7 sts in from front edge. Easing in fullness, sew on collar between markers, seam to the underside. Place markers 12 (14)cm, 4¾ (5½)in down from shoulders on back and fronts. Sew on sleeves between markers. Join side and sleeve seams.

Edging

With WS facing, using 2.50mm hook and starting at cuff, work [1dc in next st, 3 ch, miss 1 st, 1dc in next st] along edge. Noting that in places the spacing may need to be adjusted to accommodate seams, curves, etc., work this edging around remaining edges. Sew on buttons.

Idea: *make a scalloped edging in a contrasting colour.*

Using 2.50mm hook and main colour, and with RS facing, work 1 row of dc along each edge, working 1dc into each st along first and last rows, 2 dc into each tr row end and 3 dc into shaped row ends. Using 2.50mm hook and contrasting colour, and with RS facing, noting that in places the spacing may need to be adjusted to accommodate seams, curves, etc., work [1dc, 4 ch, miss 3ch] around edges. Also with RS facing, work next row: ★ss in dc, [1dc, 3 tr, 1dc] in ch sp; rep from ★, ending ss in last st.

Pompon hat

This is the easiest hat of all as it has absolutely no shaping. Simply join the top to make four points and decorate each with a different pastel-coloured pompon.

Materials

1 (1, 1, 2, 2, 2) 50g ball of Jaeger Matchmaker Merino DK in pale green and small quantities of other pastel colours
3.00mm crochet hook

Size

To fit age 3–6 months (9 months, 12 months, 18 months, 2 years, 2½ years)

Tension

21 sts and 12 rows to 10cm, 4in over tr

Abbreviations (see page 19)

Hat

Make 86 (90, 94, 98, 100, 102) ch.
ROW 1 (RS) Miss 3 ch, ★1tr in next ch; rep from ★ to end. 84 (88, 92, 96, 98, 100) sts.
Without twisting or turning the work, join with ss to top ch of 3 ch to make a ring.
Now work in rounds with RS facing:
ROUND 1 3 ch, ★1tr in next tr; rep from ★, ending with ss to top ch of 3 ch. Rep this round until a total of 20 (22, 24, 26, 28, 30) rounds has been completed.
Fasten off.

To Complete

Join ends of first row. Lay hat flat, RS out and with back join to centre. Pin the fold at each side ★★. Refold with back join to one side and pin these outer folds. The four folds should make a cross shape on top. Starting at the outside edge, join each fold with a row of dc worked through both layers (see page 18). Using pastel colours make 4 pompons and sew one to each corner of the hat top. Turn back the hat edge.

Idea: join the top of the hat straight across and add two giant curly crochet tassels, one at each side.

Tassel Hat

Materials

1 (1, 1, 2, 2, 2) balls Jaeger Matchmaker DK in lilac
3.00mm hook

To Make

Using A, work as Pompon Hat to ★★.

To Complete

With front facing and leaving a small gap at each end, join top seam with a row of dc through both layers (see page 18). Make 2 curly tassels (see below), take cord at top of tassels through small gap in top seam and stitch on inside of hat. Turn back hat edge.

Tassels

Materials

1 ball Jaeger Matchmaker Merino DK in pale blue
3.00mm hook

Size

Tassel measures approximately 9cm, 3½in long

To Make

Make 22 ch.
ROW 1 Miss first ch, 2 dc in each of next 15 ch, 1dc in each of rem 6 ch.
ROW 2 1ch, 1dc in back strand of each of next 5 sts, make 16 ch.
ROW 3 Miss first ch, 2 dc in each of next 15 ch, 1dc in back strand of each of next 6 sts.
Rep rows 2 and 3 16 times. Fasten off.
CORD
Make 10 ch, miss 1ch, 1dc in rem 9 ch. Fasten off.

To Complete

Tightly roll top of tassel around the end of the cord. With a wool needle, sew end of roll, then make stitches through to secure top and cord.

Dancing shoes

Old-fashioned bar-fastening shoes are hardly essentials for feet that aren't yet walking, but they would make a delightful present.

Materials

1 50g ball of Jaeger Matchmaker Merino 4-ply in pale green
2.00mm and 2.50mm hooks
2 small buttons

Size

To fit age 3–6 months
Actual size approximately 10cm, 4in long

Tension

25 sts and 30 rows to 10cm, 4in over dc using 2.50mm hook

Special Abbreviation (see page 19 for others)

dec 1 = decrease 1 st: [insert hook in next st, yrh, draw through loop] twice, yrh and draw through all 3 loops on hook

To Make

SOLE

Worked around a straight ch, RS facing. Mark beg of each round with contrasting yarn (see page 19).
Using 2.50mm hook, make 15 ch.
ROUND 1 Miss 2 ch, 1dc in each of next 13 ch, 2 ch, swivel work, [1dc in rem strand of next ch] 14 times, 2 ch.
ROUND 2 [1dc in each of next 14 sts, 3 dc in 2 ch sp at end] twice.
ROUND 3 [1dc in each of next 14 sts, 2 dc in each of 3 end sts] twice.
ROUND 4 [1dc in each of next 14 sts, 2 dc in each of 6 end sts] twice.
ROUND 5 [1dc in each of next 14 sts, 1dc in each of 12 end sts] twice.
ROUND 6 1dc in each of next 8 sts, 1tr in each of next 6 sts, [2 tr in next st, 1tr in next st] 6 times, 2 tr in next st, 1tr in each of next 6 sts, 1dc in each of next 7 sts, ss in next st. Fasten off.

LEFT UPPER

Starting at toe, make 7 ch.
ROW 1 (RS) Miss 2 ch, 2 dc in each of next 4 ch, 1dc in last ch. 10 sts.

ROW 2 1ch, 1dc in st below, 1dc in each of next 8 sts, 2 dc in last st. 12 sts.
ROW 3 1ch, 1dc in st below, 1dc in each st, ending 2 dc in last st. 14 sts.
Rep row 3 3 times. 20 sts. Insert marker.
ROW 7 1ch, 1dc in each of next 19 sts.
Rep row 7 5 times.
Divide for first side:
ROW 13 1ch, 1dc in each of next 5 sts, dec 1, 1dc in next st, turn. 8 sts.
ROW 14 1ch, dec 1, 1dc in each of next 5 sts. 7 sts.
Work 2 rows straight.
ROW 17 1ch, 1dc in each of next 4 sts, 2 dc in next st, 1dc in last st. 8 sts.
ROW 18 1ch, 1dc in st below, dc in each of next 7 sts. 9 sts.
Insert marker. ★★.
Work 14 rows straight. Fasten off.
2nd side:
★★★**NEXT ROW (RS)** Miss centre 2 sts, rejoin yarn, 1ch, dec 1, 1dc in each of next 6 sts. 8 sts.
NEXT ROW 1ch, 1dc in each of next 4 sts, dec 1, 1dc in last st. 7 sts.
Work 2 rows straight.
NEXT ROW 1ch, 1dc in st below, 1dc in each of next 6 sts. 8 sts.
NEXT ROW 1ch, 1dc in each of next 5 sts, 2 dc in next st, 1dc in last st. 9 sts. ★★★★.

MAKE BAR

NEXT ROW 12 ch, miss 2 ch, 1dc in each of next 10 ch, 1dc in each of next 9 ch. 20 sts.
NEXT (BUTTONHOLE) ROW 1ch, 1dc in each of next 15 sts, 2 ch, miss 2 sts, 1dc in each of next 2 sts.
Work 1 row on all 20 sts.
NEXT ROW 1ch, 1dc in each of next 8 sts, turn. 9 sts.
Cont straight on these 9 sts until 2nd side matches first side.
Fasten off.

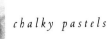
RIGHT UPPER

Work as left upper to ★★.

MAKE BAR

NEXT ROW I ch, I dc in each st, 12 ch.

NEXT ROW Miss 2 ch, I dc in each st to end. 20 sts.

NEXT (BUTTONHOLE) ROW I ch, I dc in each of next 15 sts, 2 ch, miss 2 sts, I dc in each of next 2 sts.

Work I row on all 20 sts.

NEXT ROW I ch, I dc in each of next 8 sts, turn. 9 sts.

Work 9 rows straight. Fasten off.

Cont to match left upper from ★★★ to ★★★★, then work I4 rows straight. Fasten off.

To Complete

Press, taking care not to flatten toe shaping. With right sides together, join back seam. With wrong sides together, join upper to sole with running stitch, easing in fullness at toe. Using 2.00mm hook and with upper facing, work I round dc through both upper and sole to cover stitching. Sew on buttons.

Idea: transform Dancing shoes with crochet roses.

Materials

I 25g ball of Patons Baby Pure Wool 2-ply
2.50mm hook

Rose

Work in rounds with RS facing.

Make 5 ch, ss in first ch to join into a ring.

ROUND 1 5 ch, [I tr, 2 ch] in ring 5 times, ss to 3rd ch of 5 ch.

ROUND 2 ★(I dc, I tr, 3 dtr, I tr, I dc) in ch sp; rep from ★ 5 times, ss to base of first ch.

ROUND 3 Working behind petals of round 2: 5 ch, I dc in next tr of round I, ★4ch, I dc in next tr of first round; rep from ★ 5 times, ending I dc in 3rd ch of first round.

ROUND 4 ★(I dc, 2 tr, 4 dtr, 2 tr, I dc) in ch sp; rep from ★ 5 times, ss to base of first st.

ROUND 5 Working behind petals of round 4: 6 ch, I dc in dc of round 3, ★5 ch, I dc in next dc of round 3; rep from ★ 5 times, ending I dc in first ch of round 3.

ROUND 6 ★(I dc, 2 tr, 6 dtr, 2 tr, I dc) in ch sp; rep from ★ 5 times, ss to base of first st.

Fasten off, leaving an end of approximately I0cm, 4in for attaching to the shoe.

Richard Rabbit

He's a sweet, small toy who is very easy to make. His long ears lend themselves perfectly to crochet and his pompon tail helps him to sit up.

Materials

1 50g ball of Jaeger Baby Merino DK in natural white (A), oddments of Double Knitting yarn in lilac (B) and pink (C)
3.00mm hook
Polyester stuffing

Size

Height approximately 17cm, 6½in, excluding ears

Tension

18 sts and 20 rows to 10cm, 4in over dc

Special Abbreviations (see page 19 for others)

dec 1 = decrease 1 st: [insert hook in next st, yrh and draw loop through] twice, yrh and draw through all 3 loops on hook
inc 1 = increase 1 st: work 2 dc in next st

Body

Using A, make 24 ch, join into a ring with ss in first ch.
Work in rounds with RS facing.
ROUND 1 1 ch, 1dc in next ch, inc 1, [1dc in each of next 2 ch, inc 1] 7 times. 32 sts.
Marking end of each round with contrasting yarn:
ROUNDS 2, 3, 4, 5, 6 AND 7 ★1 dc in next st; rep from ★ to end.
ROUND 8 1dc in each of next 6 sts, [dec 1] twice, 1dc in each of next 12 sts, [dec 1] twice, 1dc in each of next 6 sts. 28 sts.
ROUNDS 9, 10 AND 11 As round 2.

ROUND 12 1dc in each of next 5 sts, [dec 1] twice, 1dc in each of next 10 sts, [dec 1] twice, 1dc in each of next 5 sts. 24 sts.

ROUNDS 13, 14 AND 15 As round 2.

ROUND 16 1dc in each of next 4 sts, [dec 1] twice, 1dc in each of next 8 sts, [dec 1] twice, 1dc in each of next 4 sts. 20 sts.

ROUND 17 [Dec 1] 10 times. 10 sts. Fasten off.

Legs

Using A, make 12 ch, join into a ring with ss in first ch.
Work in rounds marking end of each round as before:

ROUND 1 1ch, 1dc in each of next 11 ch. 12 sts.

ROUNDS 2–8 ★1dc in next st; rep from ★ to end.

ROUND 9 [1dc, dec 1] 4 times. 8 sts. Fasten off.
Make 3 more the same.

Head

Using A, make 4 ch, join into a ring with ss in first ch.
Work in rounds marking end of each round as before:

ROUND 1 1ch, [inc 1 in next ch] 3 times. 7 sts.

ROUND 2 1dc in next st, [1dc in next st, inc 1] twice, 1dc in each of next 2 sts. 9 sts.

ROUND 3 1dc in each of next 3 sts, inc 1, 1dc in next st, inc 1, 1dc in each of next 3 sts. 11 sts.

ROUND 4 1dc in each of next 2 sts, [inc 1, 1dc in each of next 2 sts] 3 times. 14 sts.

ROUND 5 1dc in each of next 4 sts, 1tr in each of next 2 sts, 2 tr in each of next 2 sts, 1tr in each of next 2 sts, 1dc in each of next 4 sts. 16 sts.

ROUND 6 1dc in each of next 4 sts, 1tr in each of next 2 sts, 2 tr in each of next 4 sts, 1tr in each of next 2 sts, 1dc in each of next 4 sts. 20 sts.

ROUND 7 1dc in each of next 5 sts, 1tr in each of next 2 sts, 2 tr in each of next 6 sts, 1tr in each of next 2 sts, 1dc in each of next 5 sts. 26 sts.

ROUND 8 ★1dc in next st; rep from ★ to end.

ROUND 9 1dc in each of next 7 sts, [dec 1] 6 times, 1dc in each of next 7 sts. 20 sts.

ROUND 10 1dc in next st, dec 1, [1dc in each of next 3 sts, dec 1] 3 times, 1dc in each of next 2 sts. 16 sts.

ROUND 11 1dc in next st, [dec 1, 1dc in each of next 2 sts] 3 times, dec 1, 1dc in next st. 12 sts.

ROUND 12 1dc in next st, [dec 1, 1dc in next st] 3 times, dec 1. 8 sts.
Fasten off.

Ears

Using B, make 14 ch.
Miss 2 ch, 1dc in next ch, 1tr in each of next 8 ch, 1dc in each of next 2 ch, 3 dc in last ch, working into single rem strand of each ch, work 1dc in each of next 2 ch, 1tr in each of next 8 ch, 1dc in each of rem 2 ch.
Fasten off.
Using A, make 15 ch. Miss 3 ch, 1tr in next ch, 1dtr in each of next 8 ch, 1tr in each of next 2 ch, 3 tr in last ch, working into single rem strand of each ch, work 1tr in each of next 2 ch, 1dtr in each of next 8 ch, 1tr in each of rem 2 ch. Do not fasten off.
With RS facing, place B ear on the A ear and, taking the hook

through the corresponding st of each piece each time, work a row of dc around and through both pieces. Work 2nd ear the same.

To Complete

Stitch closed the seam at the lower edge of the body and stuff the inside with polyester stuffing. Close the top seam. Gather and stitch the lower edge of each leg, stuff, close the seam at the top and attach to the body. Using A, make a pompon for tail and stitch it on. Stuff the head; gather and stitch the opening at the back. Sew on the ears and sew the head on the body. Use C to embroider two French knots for eyes, pulling the thread firmly between them. Embroider a satin stitch nose in B.

Idea: give him a striped bow tie in soft pastels.

Materials

Double Knitting yarn in 2 colours (A and B)
3.00mm hook

Bow Tie

FIRST BAND Using A, make 16 ch. Miss 2 ch, ★1 dc in next ch; rep from ★ to end. Fasten off.

2ND BAND Using A, make 8 ch. Work as first band.

3RD BAND Using B, make 32 ch. Work first row as first band.
NEXT ROW Using A, 1 ch, ★1 dc in next st; rep from ★ to end. Fasten off.

To Complete

Join third band into a ring. Wrap second band around the centre to hide join and stitch to the centre of first band. Stitch the ends of the first band around the rabbit's neck.

Hairy hottie

Children will love this furry, friendly hot-water bottle cover. The plaid effect is achieved with brushed mohair, by making a crochet mesh and then weaving strands of yarn through it.

Materials

Capricorn Chunky Brushed Mohair in 50g balls: 1 ball each blue (A), mauve (B) and green (C)
4.50mm hook

Size

To fit a hot-water bottle approximately 20cm x 30cm, 8in x 12in, excluding stopper

Tension

7 open squares measure 10cm, 4in

Abbreviations (see page 19)

First Side

Using A, make 34 ch.
★★ **ROW 1 (RS)** Miss 5 ch, 1 tr in next ch, ★1 ch, miss 1 ch, 1 tr in next ch; rep from ★ to end. 15 open squares.
ROW 2 4 ch, ★1 tr in next tr, 1 ch; rep from ★, ending miss 1 ch, 1 tr in next ch.
Row 2 forms patt.
Patt 1 row B, 2 rows A, 2 rows C, 1 row B and 2 rows C. ★★★.
Rep 10-row stripe sequence once. Fasten off.

SHAPE TOP

NEXT ROW Miss 3 squares, join A to next st, 4 ch, [1 tr in next tr, 1 ch] 8 times, 1 tr in next tr, turn.
Cont in stripe sequence on these 9 squares until a total of 25 rows has been completed. Fasten off.

BUTTONHOLE BAND

ROW 1 With RS facing, using C, work 1 ch in first ch, then 1 dc in each ch of foundation row of first side. 31 sts.
ROW 2 1 ch, 1 dc in next st, ★3 ch, miss 3 sts, 1 dc in each of next 3 sts, rep from ★, ending 1 dc in each of next 2 sts.
ROW 3 1 ch, 1 dc in each of next 30 sts. Fasten off.

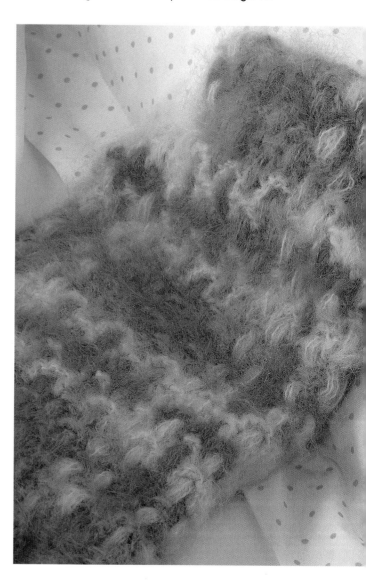

SECOND SIDE

Work as first side but omit buttonholes.

Weaving

With RS facing, pin first side to shape on ironing board and press. Without unpinning, thread a wool needle with 4 strands of B, each approximately 12cm, 5in longer than the crochet mesh. Weave these strands through the centre vertical row of open squares, leaving the ends loose. Working alternately under and over the chain bars, fill the open squares to the right with 2 rows A, 2 rows C, 1 row B and 2 rows C. Fill the squares to the left to match. Making sure that the woven strands are tensioned evenly and not too tightly, unpin and fasten off the ends on the wrong side. Weave second side to match.

To Complete

Placing right sides together, stitch sides and around the top. Turn through to right side. With left-over yarn make 5 ball buttons as for blanket trim bobbles on page 86. Sew these in place on the button band. Lightly brush the cover to fluff up texture.

Idea: use the same technique to make a handbag.

Materials

Capricorn Brushed Mohair 4-ply in 50g balls: 1 ball each bright pink (A), light blue (B) and warm pink (C)
2.50mm hook
Lining material approximately 17cm x 34cm, 6¾in x 13½in
Piping cord 28cm, 11in long

Size

Approximately 13cm, 5in square not including handle

Tension

12 open squares to 10cm, 4in

Side

Using A, make 34 ch.
Cont as for Hairy hottie from ★★ to ★★★, then work 2 rows A, 1 row B and 2 rows A. Fasten off.
Make 2.

Weaving

As for Hairy hottie but instead of fastening off the ends, machine stitch them along the edge stitch.

To Complete

Placing right sides together and leaving top edges open, join remaining 3 sides of bag. Using the crochet as a guide and adding 1cm, ⅜in seam allowance on all edges, cut out 2 squares of lining fabric. Join these along the side edges, then, leaving an opening along most of the edge, join bottom edge. Placing right sides together, insert the crochet bag inside the lining bag. Stitch around the top, leaving a small opening at each side seam for the handle. Turn bag right side out through the opening in the bottom of the lining. Stitch this closed by hand and push the lining into the bag. Make the handle by working dc with A around the piping cord. Insert 2cm at each end of the cord into the spaces left between lining and bag; secure with a few stitches.

NATURALS AND NEUTRALS

Think of winter woollies, and the creamy off-whites and earthy buffs and browns of un-dyed wool come to mind. These colours, sometimes accentuated with pastels, are ideal for outdoor clothing and cosy wraps. They blend comfortably in a nursery that combines natural wood and fleecy rugs.

Icelandic jacket

This is an interpretation in crochet of the traditional knitted Icelandic jacket with a round yoke. It's worked from the top downwards, so length is easy to adjust before the pockets are added.

Materials

Jaeger Matchmaker Merino Double Knitting in 50g balls: 3 balls natural (A), 1 ball each charcoal (B), camel (C) and pale blue (D)
3.00mm and 3.50mm hooks
6 buttons

Size

To fit age 6 months
Actual size: chest 71cm, 28in; length 28cm, 11in; sleeve 17cm, 6½in

Tension

20 sts and 12 rows to 10cm, 4in over tr using 3.50mm hook

Special Abbreviations (see page 19 for others)

dec 1 st = decrease 1 st: [yrh, insert hook in next st, yrh, draw through loop, yrh, draw through first 2 loops on hook] twice, yrh, draw through all 3 loops on hook

inc 1 = increase 1 st: work 2 tr in next st or at beg of row, 3 ch, 1 tr in st below

To Make

Worked from the top downwards.
Using 3.50mm hook and A, make 51 ch loosely.
ROW 1 (RS) Miss 3 ch, [2 tr in next ch, 1 tr in next ch] 24 times. 73 sts.
ROW 2 4 ch, [miss 2 sts, 1 dc in next st, 3 ch] 23 times, miss 2 sts, 1 dc in top ch of 3 ch. 97 sts.
ROW 3 Using B, [3 ch, 3 tr] in first ch sp, ★4 tr in next ch sp; rep from ★ to end. 96 sts.
ROW 4 Using C, 1ch, ★4 dtr in sp between 4 tr groups; rep from ★, ending 1dc in top ch of 3 ch. 94 sts.
ROW 5 Using A, 3 ch, ★1tr in next st; rep from ★ to end.
ROW 6 3 ch, 1tr in st below, 1tr in each of next 6 sts, [1tr in sp below,

1tr in each of next 8 sts] 10 times, 1tr in sp below, 1tr in each of next 6 sts, 2 tr in last st. 107 sts.
ROW 7 Using B, 1ch, 1dc in st below, 1dc in each of next 2 sts, [2 dc in next st, 1dc in each of next 8 sts] 11 times, 2 dc in next st, 1dc in each of next 4 sts. 120 sts.
ROW 8 Using D, 4 ch, ★dec 1, 1ch; rep from ★, ending 1tr in last st. 121 sts.
ROW 9 Using A, 3 ch, ★1tr in next st; rep from ★ to end.
ROW 10 3 ch, 1tr in each of next 4 sts, [2 tr in next st, 1tr in each of next 9 sts] 11 times, 2 tr in next st, 1tr in each of next 5 sts. 133 sts.
ROW 11 Using D, 1ch, ★1dc in next st; rep from ★ to end.
ROW 12 4 ch, ★ miss 2 sts, 1dc in next st, 3 ch; rep from ★, ending miss 2 sts, 1dc in 1ch.
ROW 13 Using B, [3 ch, 3 tr] in first ch sp, ★4 tr in next ch sp; rep from ★ to end.
ROW 14 Using C, 1ch, ★4 dtr in sp between 4 tr groups; rep from ★, ending 1dc in last st. 174 sts.
ROW 15 Using A, 3 ch, ★1tr in next st; rep from ★ to end.
RIGHT FRONT
ROW 1 (WS) 3 ch, 1tr in each of next 26 sts, 2 tr in next st, turn. Cont on these 29 sts only for right front.
Inc 1 st at armhole edge on next 2 rows. 31 sts.
ROW 4 6 ch, miss 3 ch, [1tr in next ch] 3 times, ★1tr in next st; rep from ★ to end. 35 sts.
ROW 5 3 ch, ★1tr in next st; rep from ★ to end.
Rep last row 15 times. Fasten off.
RIGHT SLEEVE
ROW 1 (WS) Using 3.50mm hook rejoin A at st nearest to right front, 3 ch, 1tr in st below, 1tr in each of next 28 sts, 2 tr in next st, turn. 32 sts.
★★ Inc 1 st at each end of next 2 rows.
ROW 4 6 ch, miss 3 ch, [1tr in next ch] 3 times, ★1tr in next st; rep from ★ to end, [1dtr in base of previous st] 4 times. 44 sts.

ROW 5 3 ch, ★ l tr in next st; rep from ★ to end. ★★★.

DEC ROW 3 ch, dec 1, ★ l tr in next st; rep from ★ to last 3 sts, dec 1, l tr in last st.

Dec thus at each end of every 3rd row until 34 sts rem.

Work 2 rows straight.

NEXT ROW 3 ch, l tr in each of next 3 sts, [dec 1, l tr in each of next 4 sts] 5 times. 29 sts. Fasten off.

BACK

ROW 1 (WS) Using 3.50mm hook rejoin A at st nearest to right sleeve, 3 ch, l tr in st below, l tr in each of next 56 sts, 2 tr in next st, turn. 60 sts.

Work as right sleeve from ★★ to ★★★. 72 sts.

Rep row 5 15 times. Fasten off.

LEFT SLEEVE

ROW 1 (WS) Using 3.50mm hook rejoin A at st nearest to back, work as right sleeve.

LEFT FRONT

ROW 1 (WS) Using 3.50mm hook and A, rejoin yarn at st nearest to left sleeve, 3 ch, l tr in st below, ★ l tr in next st; rep from ★ to end. 29 sts.

Inc 1 st at armhole edge on next 2 rows. 31 sts.

NEXT ROW 3 ch, ★ l tr in next st; rep from ★ to end, [l dtr in base of previous st] 4 times. 35 sts.

Complete to match right front.

Pockets

Using 3.50mm hook and A, make 22 ch.

ROW 1 (RS) Miss 3 ch, ★ l tr in next ch; rep from ★ to end. 20 sts.

ROW 2 3 ch, ★ l tr in next st; rep from ★ to end.

Rep row 2 8 times. Do not fasten off.

Make 2.

Edging

With RS facing and using 3.00mm hook, work 1 round of dc, working 1 st in each st at top and bottom, 3 sts in each corner and 2 sts in each row end st. Still with RS facing, work 1 round of crab stitch (dc worked from left to right; see page 14). Fasten off.

Front edging and neckband

With RS facing, using 3.00mm hook and A and working 2 sts in each tr row end, work in dc up right front, 3 dc in corner, 1 dc in each st around neck, 3 dc in 2nd corner, work in dc down left front to match right front.

Using D, work 1 row dc.

With contrasting yarn mark position of 6 buttonholes on right front, each buttonhole 3 sts wide.

NEXT ROW Work in dc, working each buttonhole [3 ch, miss 3 sts] and working 2 dc in each corner.

NEXT ROW Work in dc throughout, working 1 dc in each ch of each buttonhole and 2 dc in each corner.

Using B, work 1 row dc.

Fasten off.

To Complete

Press. Join underarm seams. Join side and sleeve seams.

CUFFS

With RS facing, using 3.00mm hook and D, work 3 rounds of dc, then using B, work 1 round of dc. Fasten off.

Idea: create a little scarf in matching colours.

Materials

Jaeger Matchmaker Merino Double Knitting: 1 ball natural (A) and oddments in pale blue (B), charcoal (C) and camel (D)
3.50mm hook

LOWER EDGE

With RS facing, using 3.00mm hook and A, work 1 row of crab stitch. Using running stitch and working on RS inner line of crab stitch, sew on pockets. Sew on buttons.

Size

Length approximately 60cm, 23½in

To Make

Worked in 2 halves, starting at the centre.
Using A, make 24 ch, join into a ring with ss in first ch.
Now work in rounds with RS facing.
ROUND 1 3 ch, ★1tr in next ch; rep from ★ to end, ss around 3 ch. 24 sts.
★★ **ROUND 2** 3 ch, ★1tr in next st; rep from ★ to end, ss around 3 ch.
Rep round 2 24 times.
ROUND 27 Using B, work as round 2.
ROUND 28 Using C, 1ch, ★1dc in next st; rep from ★ to end, ss to 1ch.
ROUND 29 Using A, work as round 2.
ROUND 30 Using D, work as round 28.
ROUND 31 ★ Miss 1 st, 7 tr in next st, miss 1 st, 1dc in next st; rep from ★ to end, ss to top of first tr. Fasten off.
NEXT ROUND With RS facing, using A, rejoin yarn to beg of round 1, 3 ch, working in remaining strand of each ch of 23 foundation ch, work 1tr in each ch. 24sts.
Complete as first half from ★★.

Granny's favourite

Noone knows whose granny invented so-called granny squares, but these motifs are enjoyable, easy crochet with lots of scope for playing with colour. Here, a single pastel colour has been included in each square of naturals and the last round has been worked in off-white.

Materials

Double Knitting yarn in naturals ranging from off-white to brown and in smaller quantities of pastel colours

3.00 and 3.50mm hook

A = fiirst colour of square
B = second colour of square
C = third colour of square
D = fourth colour of square

Size

The blanket shown uses 63 squares and measures 56cm x 72cm, 22in x 28¼in, excluding edging

Tension

Each square measures approximately 8cm, 3¼in worked with 3.50mm hook

Special Abbreviation (see page 19 for others)

lp = picot: 4 ch, 1dc in first of 4 ch

To Make

The square is worked in rounds, with the RS facing on all rounds. Using 3.50mm hook and A, make 5 ch, ss into first ch to form a ring.

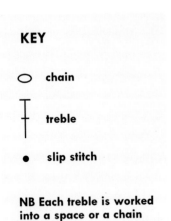

KEY

◯ chain

┬ treble

● slip stitch

NB Each treble is worked into a space or a chain space and not into a stitch

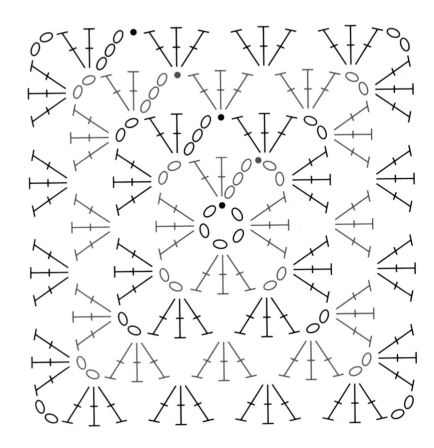

ROUND 1 With A, make 3 ch, into ring work 2 tr, 2 ch, ★3 tr, 2 ch; rep from ★ twice, ss into top ch of 3 ch. Fasten off.

ROUND 2 Join B to 2 ch sp with ss, (3 ch, 2 tr, 2 ch, 3 tr) in same sp, ★ into next ch sp work (3 tr, 2 ch, 3 tr); rep from ★ twice, ss into top ch of 3 ch. Fasten off.

ROUND 3 Join C to 2 ch sp with ss, (3 ch, 2 tr, 2 ch, 3 tr), in same sp, work 3 tr in sp between 3 tr groups, ★ (3 tr, 2 ch, 3 tr) into next ch sp, 3 tr in sp between 3 tr groups; rep from ★ twice more, ss into top ch of 3 ch. Fasten off.

ROUND 4 Join D to 2 ch sp with ss, (3 ch, 2 tr, 2 ch, 3 tr) in same sp, [3 tr in sp between 3 tr groups] twice, ★ (3 tr, 2 ch, 3 tr) in next ch sp, [3 tr in sp between 3 tr groups] twice; rep from ★ twice, ss into top ch of 3 ch. Fasten off.

To Complete

Pin out each square and press (see page 18). Placing right sides together and using 3.00mm hook and D, join the squares with dc (see page 18). Join strips of 8 squares for the length of the blanket, then work in rows across to join the 7 strips.

Edging

With RS facing and using 3.50mm hook and D, work in rounds:

ROUND 1 Join in corner ch sp, 4 ch, 1dc in same ch sp, ★3 ch, 1dc in next sp; rep from ★ to next corner, (1dc, 3 ch, 1dc) in corner sp. Work rem 3 sides the same, ending with ss in first ch.

ROUND 2 Into new corner ch sp work (2 dc, 1 p, 2 dc), into each ch sp work (2 dc, 1 p, 2 dc), ending with ss in first dc. Fasten off.

Idea: use identical squares to make building blocks.

Materials

FOR ONE BLOCK

Double Knitting yarn in four colours – one pastel and three natural shades
3.00mm and 3.50mm hooks
10cm, ⅛yd lining fabric
Piece of cardboard 8cm x 48cm, 3¼in x 19½in, or equivalent area
Polyester stuffing
Sewing needle and thread

A = pastel colour
B = dark natural
C = medium-tone natural
D = light natural

Tension

Each square measures approximately 8cm, 3¼in

To Make

Using 3.50mm hook, make 6 squares as for Granny's favourite.

To Complete

Pin out each square and press (see page 18). Use one square to cut 6 same-size squares from cardboard and 6 lining fabric squares, adding 1cm, ½in seam allowance on all edges. Stitch together the fabric squares to make a block, leaving open 2 adjoining sides. Insert the cardboard to stiffen the sides, and fill the centre with stuffing. Stitch the remaining seams. Using 3.00mm hook and D and placing WS together, join 2 crochet squares along one edge with dc (see page 18). In the same way, attach 2 more squares to make a strip, then join the first and last squares to make a ring. Still working on the right side and matching corners carefully, attach the fifth square to the ring to make an open box. Insert the lining fabric block and complete the crochet block by attaching the remaining crochet square in the same way as before.

Whirligig beret

Crochet lends itself to motifs of every kind, as here, where a hexagon motif has been extended to make a stylish beret. This hexagon could be used as the basis of any hat — simply continue straight once the increases fit the crown of the head and you will have a pull-on style.

Materials
Jaeger Matchmaker Merino DK in 50g balls: 1 (1, 2) balls natural (A), 1 ball each charcoal (B), camel (C) and pale blue (D)
3.00mm and 3.50mm hooks

Size
To fit age 12 months (18 months, 2 years)

Tension
20 sts and 11 rows to 10cm. 4in over tr with 3.50mm hook

Special abbreviation (see page 19 for others)
dec 1 = decrease 1 st: [yrh, insert hook in next st and draw loop through, yrh and draw through first 2 loops] twice, yrh and draw through remaining 3 loops

To Make
Worked in rounds with right side facing. Using 3.50mm hook and A, make 4 ch, join into a ring with ss in first ch.
ROUND 1 3 ch, 11 tr in ring, ss to top ch of 3 ch, 12 sts.
ROUND 2 4 ch, ★ miss next tr, 1 dc in next tr, 3 ch; rep from ★ 4 times, miss last tr, ss in first of 4 ch.
ROUND 3 Using B, (3 ch, 4 tr) in first sp, ★5 tr in next sp; rep from ★ 4 times, ss to top ch of 3 ch.
ROUND 4 Using C, (4 ch, 6 dtr) in sp between first two 5 tr groups, ★7 dtr in next sp between 5 tr groups; rep from ★ 4 times, ss in top ch of 4 ch.
ROUND 5 Using A, (4 ch, 1tr) in centre dtr of group, ★1tr in each of next 6 sts, (1tr, 1ch, 1tr) in centre dtr of group; rep from ★ 4 times, 1tr in each of next 6 sts, ss to 3rd of 4 ch, ss into sp.

ROUND 6 (4 ch, 1tr) in sp below, ★1 tr in each of next 8 sts, (1tr, 1tr) in ch sp; rep from ★ 4 times, 1tr in each of next 8 sts, ss to 3rd of 4 ch, ss into sp.
ROUND 7 Using B, (2 ch, 1dc) in ch sp below, ★1dc in each of next 10 sts, (1dc, 1ch, 1dc) in next ch sp; rep from ★ 4 times, 1dc in each of next 10 sts, ss to first ch of 2 ch.
ROUND 8 Using D, (4 ch, 1tr) in ch sp below, ★ [1ch, dec 1] 6 times, 1ch, (1tr, 1ch, 1tr) in ch sp; rep from ★ 4 times, [1ch, dec 1] 6 times, 1ch, ss to 3rd of 4 ch, ss into sp.
ROUND 9 Using A, (4 ch, 1tr) in ch sp below, ★ [1tr in next ch sp, 1tr in dec] 6 times, 1tr in next ch sp, (1tr, 1ch, 1tr) in corner ch sp; rep from ★ 4 times, [1tr in next ch sp, 1tr in dec] 6 times, 1tr in next ch sp, ss to 3rd of 4 ch, ss into sp.
ROUND 10 (4 ch, 1tr) in ch sp below, ★1tr in each of next 15 sts, (1tr, 1ch, 1tr) in ch sp; rep from ★ 4 times, 1tr in each of next 15 sts, ss to 3rd of 4 ch, ss into sp.
ROUND 11 (4 ch, 1tr) in ch sp below, ★1tr in each of next 17 sts, (1tr, 1ch, 1tr) in ch sp; rep from ★ 4 times, 1tr in each of next 17 sts, ss to 3rd of 4 ch, ss into sp.
Working 2 more tr between each pair of incs, rep 11th round 0 (1, 2) times.
NEXT ROUND 3 ch, ★1tr in each of next 19 (21, 23) tr, 1tr in ch sp; rep from ★ 4 times, 1tr in each of next 19 (21, 23) tr, ss to top ch of 3 ch.
NEXT ROUND 3 ch, ★1tr in next st; rep from ★ to end, ss to top ch of 3 ch. Rep last round 2 (3, 4) times.
NEXT ROUND 3 ch, dec 1, ★1tr, dec 1; rep from ★ to end, ss to top ch of 3 ch.
NEXT ROUND Using 3.00mm hook and D, 1ch, ★1dc in next st; rep from ★ to end, ss to ch.
Rep last round twice, then work 1 round with B. Fasten off.

Sea boot bootees

These sturdy little bootees in creamy white wool were inspired by fishermen's long sea boot stockings. They're made entirely in double crochet worked from the top. The ribbed effect on the band, heel and toe is achieved by working into the back of the stitch.

Materials
1 50g ball of Jaeger Baby Merino 4-ply in off-white
3.00mm hook

Size
To fit age 6 months
Bootee foot approximately 11cm, 4¼in long

Tension
25 sts and 28 rows to 10cm, 4in over dc

Special Abbreviation (see page 19 for others)
dec 1 = decrease 1 st: [insert hook in next st, yrh, draw through loop] twice, yrh, draw through all 3 loops on hook

To Make
Start with band at top.
Make 11 ch
ROW 1 (RS) Miss 2 ch, 1dc in each of next 9 ch. 10 sts.
ROW 2 1ch, ★ 1dc in back strand of next st; rep from ★, ending 1dc in ch.

Idea: combine two colours in a thicker, luxury yarn and you will have a Christmas stocking to treasure

Materials
Debbie Bliss Cashmerino Aran: 1 50g ball each pale blue (A) and olive (B)
4.50mm hook

Size
Foot length approximately 17cm, 6¾in

Tension
15 sts and 20 rows to 10cm, 4in over dc

To Make
This is worked like the Sea boot bootees, except that the band, heel and toe are worked with A and the rest of the bootee with B. When working into the ends of rows – around the band for the main part and around the heel for the foot – work first round or row in A then cont with B. This gives a neat colour change.

Row 2 forms ridge pattern.

Rep row 2 until a total of 36 rows has been completed. 18 ridges. Fasten off.

Join the 2 short ends to form a band.

MAIN PART

Starting at seam with RS facing and working into both strands of each dc, 1ch, 1dc in first ridge, then 2 dc in each ridge to make a total of 36 sts, join with ss to ch.

Marking rounds (see page 19), work a total of 14 continuous rounds dc, then work 10 sts of next round, turn.

HEEL

Make 1ch, 1dc in back strand of each of next 15dc, turn.

Cont in rows, working into back strand of each dc, on these 16 sts. Work 10 rows straight.

NEXT ROW (RS) 1ch, 1dc in each of next 5 sts, [dec 1] twice, 1dc in each of rem 6 sts.

NEXT ROW 1ch, 1dc in each of next 4 sts, [dec 1] twice, 1dc in each of rem 5 sts.

Working 1 st less at each end, cont to dec twice in centre of every row until 6 sts rem.

NEXT ROW Miss first st, [dec 1] twice, miss last st. Fasten off.

Rejoin yarn and, with RS facing and working in both strands of every dc, work 1dc in each of 20 sts of front, 12 dc along first side of heel and 12dc in 2nd side of heel. 44 sts.

Cont in rounds

NEXT ROUND Dec 1, 1dc in each of next 16 sts, [dec 1] twice, 1dc in each of next 20 sts, dec 1. 40 sts.

Work 1 round.

NEXT ROUND Dec 1, 1dc in each of next 14 sts, [dec 1] twice, 1dc in each of next 18 sts, dec 1. 36 sts.

Work 1 round straight.

TOE SHAPING

★★ **NEXT ROW** 1dc in each of next 18 sts, turn.

Cont in rows, working in back strand of each dc.

ROW 1 1ch, 1dc in each of next 17 sts, turn.

ROW 2 1ch, dec 1, 1dc in each of next 12 sts, dec 1, 1dc in last st. 16 sts.

Cont to dec 1 st in from each end of every RS row until 8 sts rem. Fasten off.

NEXT ROW (RS) Rejoin yarn to rem 18 sts of foot. Work as previous section from ★★.

To Complete

Join seam around toe.

Barnaby Bear

He's a thoroughly old-fashioned teddy in every respect, appealing to young and old alike. Simple shapings are used to produce a friendly face and a dumpy body. He's only marginally more complicated to make than his friend Richard Rabbit.

Materials

Jaeger Matchmaker Merino Double Knitting in 50g balls: 2 balls camel (A) and 1 ball natural (B)
3.00mm hook
Oddments of Double Knitting or embroidery wool in brown
Polyester stuffing

Size

Approximately 26cm, 10¼in high

Tension

18 sts and 20 rows to 10cm, 4in over dc

Special Abbreviations (see page 19 for others)

dec 1 = decrease 1 st: [insert hook in next st, yrh, draw through loop] twice, yrh, draw through all 3 loops on hook
inc 1 = increase 1 st: work 2 dc in next st

Ears

Using B, make 5 ch.
ROW 1 (RS) Miss 2 ch, 5 dc in next ch, miss 1 ch, ss to last ch.
ROW 2 1 ch, [inc 1] 5 times, 1 dc in ch. 12 sts.
ROW 3 1 ch, inc 1, 1 dc in next st, inc 1, 1 dc in each of next 4 sts, [inc 1, 1 dc in next st] twice. 16 sts. Fasten off.
Using B, make 2nd shape the same, then with A, make 2 more.
To join front of ear to back, place 1 shape B on 1 shape A, WS together: using A, and with B side facing, taking hook through the corresponding st of each shape each time, work a row of dc around and through both pieces. Make 2nd ear in the same way.

Muzzle

Using A, make 3 ch.

Work in rounds with RS facing and mark end of each round with contrasting yarn.
ROUND 1 Miss 2 ch, 8 dc in next ch. 9 sts.
ROUND 2 [Inc 1, 1 dc in each of next 2 sts] 3 times. 12 sts.
ROUND 3 [Inc 1, 1 dc in each of next 3 sts] 3 times. 15 sts.
ROUND 4 [Inc 1, 1 dc in each of next 4 sts] 3 times. 18 sts.
Cont to inc thus, working 1 st more after each inc, until 7th round has been completed. 27 sts. Ss in next st. Fasten off.

Head

Using A, ch 3.
Working in rounds, as before:
ROUND 1 Miss 2 ch, 7 dc in next ch. 8 sts.
ROUND 2 [Inc 1, 1 dc in next st] 4 times. 12 sts.
ROUND 3 [Inc 1, 1 dc in each of next 2 sts] 4 times. 16 sts.
ROUND 4 [Inc 1, 1 dc in each of next 3 sts] 4 times. 20 sts. ★★.
Cont to inc thus, working 1 st more after each inc, until 11th round has been completed. 48 sts.
Work 6 rounds straight.
ROUND 18 Make slots for ears: 1 dc in each of next 14 sts, 5 ch, miss 5 sts, 1 dc in each of next 10 sts, 5 ch, miss 5 sts, 1 dc in each of next 14 sts.
ROUND 19 1 dc in each dc and each ch.
Work 1 more round straight.
ROUND 21 [Dec 1, 1 dc in each of next 6 sts] 6 times. 42 sts.
ROUND 22 [Dec 1, 1 dc in each of next 5 sts] 6 times. 36 sts.
Cont to dec thus, working 1 st less after each dec, until 26th round has been completed. 12 sts. Fasten off, leaving an end long enough to work 1 more round.
Gather base of each ear, set ears in slots and sew on firmly. Stuff the head and muzzle. Sew on muzzle, setting it low on the head. Embroider the nose with satin stitch and the eyes with French knots,

pulling the yarn between the two quite firmly.

Close the back of the head:

LAST ROUND [Dec 1] 6 times. 6 sts. Fasten off. Use yarn end to gather and secure these sts.

Body

Using A, make 3 ch.

Work in rounds, as before:

ROUND 1 Miss 2 ch, 5 dc in next ch. 6 sts.

ROUND 2 [Inc 1] 6 times. 12 sts.

ROUND 3 [Inc 1, 1dc in next st] 6 times. 18 sts.

ROUND 4 [Inc 1, 1dc in each of next 2 sts] 6 times. 24 sts.

Cont to inc thus, working 1 st more after each inc, until 8th round has been completed. 48 sts.

Work 6 rounds straight.

ROUND 15 [Dec 1, 1dc in each of next 10 sts] 4 times. 44 sts.

Work 4 rounds straight.

ROUND 20 [Dec 1, 1dc in each of next 9 sts] 4 times. 40 sts.

Work 4 rounds straight.

ROUND 25 [Dec 1, 1dc in each of next 8 sts] 4 times. 36 sts.

Work 4 rounds straight. Fasten off. Join 1cm, ½in at each side for shoulders.

Stuff body and sew on head.

Arm

Using A, work as beg of head to ★★.

Work 7 rounds straight.

ROUND 12 [Dec 1, 1dc in each of next 3 sts] 4 times. 16 sts.

Work 7 rounds straight.

ROUND 20 [Dec 1, 1dc in each of next 2 sts] 4 times. 12 sts.

Work 3 rounds straight.

ROUND 24 [Dec 1] 6 times. 6 sts. Fasten off. Make 2nd arm the same.

Foot

Begin with sole.

Using B, make 9 ch.

Work around this straight ch, RS facing and marking end of each of each round with contrasting yarn:

ROUND 1 Miss 2 ch, 1dc in each of next 7 ch. 8 sts. 2 ch, 1dc in rem strand of each of next 8 ch, 2 ch.

ROUND 2 1dc in each of next 8 sts, 3 dc in ch sp, 1dc in each of next 8 sts, 3 dc in ch sp.

ROUND 3 1dc in each of next 8 sts, inc 1 in each of 3 end sts, 1dc in each of next 8 sts, inc 1 in each of 3 end sts.

ROUND 4 1dc in each of next 8 sts, inc 1 in each of 6 end sts, 1dc in each of next 8 sts, inc 1 in each of 6 end sts. 40 sts. Ss in next st. Fasten off.

ROUND 5 With A, 1ch in next st, 1dc in each of next 38 sts, 1dc in ss, join with ss in ch. Fasten off.

MAIN PART OF FOOT

Using A, make 7 ch.

ROW 1 (RS) Miss 2 ch, inc 1, 1dc in each of next 2 ch, inc 1, 1dc in last ch. 8 sts.

ROW 2 1ch, inc 1, 1dc in each of next 4 sts, inc 1, 1dc in ch. 10 sts.

ROW 3 1ch, inc 1, 1dc in each of next 6 sts, inc 1, 1dc in ch. 12 sts.

ROW 4 1ch, inc 1, 1dc in each of next 2 sts, [inc 1] 4 times, 1dc in each of next 2 sts, inc 1, 1dc in ch. 18 sts.

ROW 5 1ch, inc 1, 1dc in each of next 3 sts, [dec 1] 4 times, 1dc in each of next 3 sts, inc 1, 1dc in ch. 16 sts.

Work 5 rows straight.

NEXT ROW 1ch, 1dc in each of next 5 sts, turn.

Cont on these 6 sts only for first side. Work 7 rows straight. Fasten off.

NEXT ROW With RS facing, miss centre 4 sts, rejoin yarn, 1ch, 1dc in each of next 5 sts.

Work 7 rows straight on these 6 sts. Fasten off. Make 2nd foot the same.

Leg

Join back seam of foot. Using A, with RS facing and starting at seam, work 8 dc along side, 4 dc across front and 8 dc along 2nd side, join with ss. 20 sts.

Work in rounds with RS facing.

NEXT ROUND Dec 1, 1dc in each of next 5 sts, dec 1, 1dc in each of next 2 sts, dec 1, 1dc in each of next 5 sts, dec 1. 16 sts.

Work 4 rounds straight.

NEXT ROUND [Inc 1, 1dc in each of next 3 sts] 4 times. 20 sts.

Work 6 rounds straight.

NEXT ROUND [Inc 1, 1dc in each of next 4 sts] 4 times. 24 sts.

Work 2 rounds straight.

NEXT ROUND [Dec 1, 1dc in each of next 2 sts] 6 times. 18 sts.
NEXT ROUND [Dec 1, 1dc in next st] 6 times. 12 sts
NEXT ROUND [Dec 1] 6 times. 6 sts. Fasten off. Make 2nd leg the same.

Idea: why not give him a tiny waistcoat?

Materials
Small amount of Double Knitting yarn
3.00mm hook

Special Abbreviation (see page 19 for others)
dec 1 = decrease 1 st: [yrh, insert hook in next st, yrh, draw through loop, yrh, draw through first 2 loops on hook] twice, yrh, draw through all 3 loops on hook

To Complete
Pin sole in place on foot, RS outwards. Using A, and with sole uppermost, work a row of dc around foot through both layers of crochet, easing in fullness. Stuff arms and legs. Gather at top and sew in position firmly.

To Make
Make 49 ch.
ROW 1 Miss 3 ch, ★1tr in next ch; rep from ★ to end. 47 sts.
ROW 2 3 ch, ★1tr in next st; rep from ★ to end.
ROW 3 3 ch, 1tr in each of next 5 sts, dec 1, 1tr in each of next 6 sts, dec 1, 1tr in each of next 15 sts, dec 1, 1tr in each of next 6 sts, dec 1, 1tr in each of next 6 sts. 43 sts.
ROW 4 3 ch, 1tr in each of next 5 sts, dec 1, 1tr in each of next 4 sts, dec 1, 1tr in each of next 15 sts, dec 1, 1tr in each of next 4 sts, dec 1, 1tr in each of next 6 sts. 39 sts.
ROW 5 3 ch, 1tr in each of next 5 sts, dec 1, 1tr in each of next 2 sts, dec 1, 1tr in each of next 15 sts, dec 1, 1tr in each of next 2 sts, dec 1, 1tr in each of next 6 sts. 35 sts.
ROW 6 3 ch, 1tr in each of next 3 sts, turn.
Work 2 rows straight on these 4 sts. Fasten off.
NEXT ROW Miss next 6 sts, rejoin yarn, 3 ch, 1tr in each of next 14 sts, turn.
Work 2 rows straight on these 15 sts. Fasten off.
NEXT ROW Miss next 6 sts, rejoin yarn, 3 ch, 1tr in each of next 3 sts. Work 2 rows straight on these 4 sts. Fasten off.

To Complete
Join shoulder seams. Around each edge work 1 row dc, followed by 1 row crab stitch (dc worked from left to right; see page 14).

PAINTBOX COLOURS

Clear, bright colours have an immediacy that appeals to little extroverts. Try putting two or more of them together – red with purple or lime green with acid yellow, for example. This sort of colour combining has been happening around the world for centuries, but it always looks fresh and exciting.

Mexican jacket

Influenced by Latin America, this chunky jacket is banded with strong stripes which are, in turn, patterned with criss-cross motifs. It's all in straightforward double crochet, including the shawl collar.

Materials

Rowan Wool Cotton in 50g balls: 3 (3, 4) balls bright blue (A); 1 ball each turquoise (B), lilac (C), raspberry (D) and lime (E)
3.50mm and 4.00mm hooks
3 buttons

Size

To fit ages 12 months (18 months, 2 years)
Actual size: chest 60 (65, 70)cm, 23½ (25½, 27½)in; length 28 (32, 36)cm, 11 (12½, 14)in; sleeve 17 (20, 23)cm, 6½ (7¾, 9)in

Tension

17 sts and 20 rows to 10cm, 4in over dc using 4.00mm hook

Special Abbreviations (see page 19 for others)

dec 1 = decrease 1 st: [insert hook in next st, yrh, draw loop through] twice, yrh, draw through all 3 loops on hook
inc 1 = increase 1 st: work 2 dc in next st

Note: When changing colour on motifs, work the first half of the stitch in the first colour and the second half of the stitch in the second colour (see pages 17–18).

Back

Using 4.00mm hook and A, make 52 (56, 60) ch.
ROW 1 (RS) Miss 2 ch, ★1dc in next ch; rep from ★ to end. 51 (55, 59) sts.
ROW 2 1ch, ★1dc in next dc; rep from ★, ending 1dc in ch.
Rep row 2 to make a total of 16 (20, 24) rows.
Work 2 rows B and 1 row A.
Now patt from chart (see page 83) thus:
ROW 1 (WS) Using B, 1ch, 1dc in each of next 13 (15, 17) sts, reading

row 1 of chart from right to left, dc 6 C, 11 B, 6 C, work rem 14 (16, 18) dc with B.
ROW 2 Using B, 1ch, 1dc in each of next 14 (16, 18) sts, reading row 2 of chart from left to right, dc 6 C, 9 B, 6 C, work rem 15 (17, 19) sts with B.
Cont to patt thus from chart, working sts at either side of chart sts in B on rows 3 to 6, in A on row 7 and in D on rows 8 to 13.
Work 1 row A and 2 rows D.
Cont with A for 21 (25, 29) rows. Fasten off.

Left Front

Using 4.00mm hook and A, make 20 (22, 24) ch.
ROW 1 (RS) Miss 2 ch, 1dc in each of next 16 (18, 20) ch, 2 dc in next ch, 1dc in next ch. 20 (22, 24) sts.
ROW 2 1ch, 2 dc in next st, ★1dc in next st; rep from ★, ending 1dc in ch.
ROW 3 1ch, ★1dc in next st; rep from ★ to last 2 sts, 2 dc in next st, 1dc in ch.
Rep last 2 rows once, then inc at front edge on RS rows 5 times. 29 (31, 33) sts.
Work 1 (5, 9) rows straight, thus completing 16 (20, 24) rows.
Work 2 rows B and 1 row A.
Now patt from chart thus:
ROW 1 (WS) Using B, 1ch, 1dc in each of next 2 (3, 4) sts; reading row 1 of chart from right to left, dc 6 C, 11 B, 6 C, work rem 3 (4, 5) dc with B.
Cont to patt thus from chart until row 13 of chart has been completed, working sts at either side of chart sts as back.
Work 1 row A and 2 rows D.
NECK SHAPING
ROW 1 (WS) Using A, 1ch, dec 1, 1dc in each st, 1dc in ch.
ROW 2 Using A, 1ch, 1dc in each st to last 3 sts, dec 1, 1dc in ch.

Cont with A, dec I st at front edge on next 3 (5, 7) rows, then on WS rows 5 (4, 3) times. 19 (20, 21) sts.

Cont straight until front matches back to shoulder. Fasten off.

Right Front

Using hook and A, make 20 (22, 24) ch.

ROW 1 (RS) Miss 2 ch, 2 dc in next ch, I dc in each of next 17 (19, 21) ch. 20 (22, 24) sts.

ROW 2 I ch, ★I dc in next st; rep from ★ to last 2 sts, 2 dc in next st, I dc in ch.

ROW 3 I ch, 2 dc in next st, ★I dc in next st; rep from ★, ending I dc in ch.

Rep last 2 rows once, then inc at front edge on RS rows 5 times. 29 (31, 33) sts.

Work I (5, 9) rows straight, thus completing 16 (20, 24) rows.

1ST BUTTONHOLE ROW (RS) Using B, I ch, I dc in each of next 2 sts, 2 ch, miss 2 sts, ★I dc in next st; rep from ★, ending I dc in ch.

2ND BUTTONHOLE ROW With B, I ch, I dc in each of next 28 (30, 32) sts.

Work I row A.

Now patt from chart, working 2nd buttonhole on rows 6 and 7 of chart, until row 13 of chart has been completed.

Working 3rd buttonhole on next 2 rows, work I row A and 2 rows D.

NECK SHAPING

Using A, dec I st in from front edge, work to match left front. Complete to match left front.

Sleeves

Using 4.00mm hook and A, make 26 (28, 30) ch.

ROW 1 (RS) As row I of back. 25 (27, 29) sts.

ROW 2 As row 2 of back.

ROW 3 I ch, inc I, ★I dc in next st; rep from ★ to last 2 sts, inc I, I dc in ch.

Cont to inc thus on every foll 4th row until a total of 16 (22, 28) rows has been completed.

Inc as before, work 2 rows B and I row A. 35 (39, 45) sts.

Now patt from chart thus:

ROW 1 (WS) Using B, I ch, I dc in each of next 5 (7, 10) sts, reading row I of chart from right to left, dc 6 C, 11 B, 6 C, work rem 6 (8, 11) dc with B.

Inc I st at each end of row 4 (2, 4) and for 2nd and 3rd sizes only inc I st at each end of row (6, 8), cont to patt until row 13 of chart has been completed. 37 (43, 49) sts. Work I row A and 2 rows D. Fasten off.

Collar

Worked from centre back neck.

Using 4.00mm hook and A, make 14 (16, 18) ch.

ROW 1 (RS) As first row of back. 13 (15, 17) sts. ★★.

ROW 2 As row 2 of back.

Rep this row until there is a total of 32 (34, 36) rows. ★★★.

DEC ROW (RS) I ch, dec I, ★I dc in next st; rep from ★ to end.

Cont to dec I st in from this edge on next 4 RS rows, then dec in same way on every row until 3 sts rem.

NEXT ROW I ch, dec I. Fasten off.

NEXT ROW With RS facing and working into rem strand of each ch of foundation ch, work 13 (15, 17) dc.

Work as first part of collar from ★★ to ★★★.

DEC ROW (RS) I ch, ★I dc in next st; rep from ★ to last 3 sts, dec I, I dc in ch.

Complete to match first part.

To Complete

Press. Join shoulder seams. With right sides together, easing fullness around back neck, sew on collar, finishing at start of neck shaping. Sew on sleeves, matching stripes at underarms. Join side and sleeve seams. With right side facing, using 3.50mm hook and A, beg at start of neck shaping on left front, work a row of dc down left front, along lower edge, then up right front to start of neck shaping. Fasten off. Sew on buttons.

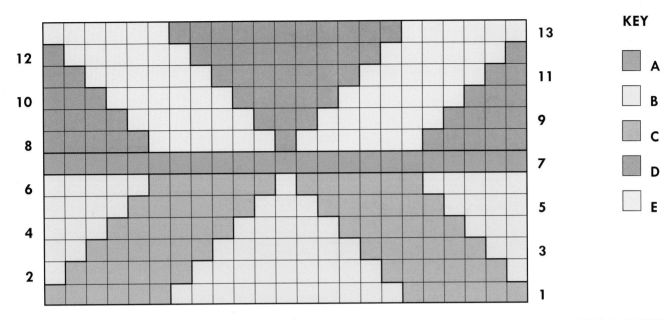

KEY

◻	A
◻	B
◻	C
◻	D
◻	E

Harlequin blanket

The squares of this bright patchwork are made up of pairs of triangles, which give the design a strongly diagonal look. Here again, all the joining is done with crochet.

Materials

Double Knitting yarn in as many bright colours as possible
3.50mm hook

Size

2 triangles joined measure approximately 11cm, 4¼in square
The blanket shown comprises 48 squares and measures 66cm × 88cm, 26in × 34¼in

Tension

Approximately 20 sts and 10 rows to 10cm, 4in over tr

Abbreviations (see page 19)

Triangle

ROW 1 (RS) 4 ch, 3 tr in first ch. 4 sts.
ROW 2 3 ch, 1 tr in st below, 1 tr in each of next 2 tr, 2 tr in 4th ch. 6 sts.

ROW 3 3 ch, 2 tr in st below, 1 tr in each of next 4 tr, 3 tr in 3rd ch. 10 sts.
ROW 4 3 ch, 1 tr in st below, 1 tr in each of next 8 tr, 2 tr in 3rd ch. 12 sts.
ROW 5 3 ch, 2 tr in st below, 1 tr in each of next 10 tr, 3 tr in 3rd ch. 16 sts.
ROW 6 3 ch, 1 tr in st below, 1 tr in each of next 14 tr, 2 tr in 3rd ch. 18 sts.
ROW 7 3 ch, 2 tr in st below, 1 tr in each of next 16 tr, 3 tr in 3rd ch. 22 sts.
ROW 8 3 ch, 1 tr in st below, 1 tr in each of next 20 tr, 2 tr in 3rd ch. 24 sts.
ROW 9 (EDGING ON 2 SHAPED SIDES OF TRIANGLE) 1 ch, work into edge sts: 1 dc in first st, 2 dc in each of next 7 row ends, 2 dc in corner ch, 2 dc in each of next 8 row ends. Fasten off.

KEY

⬯ chain

✚ double crochet

⊤ treble

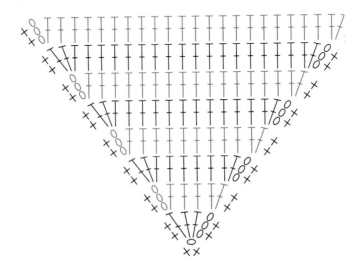

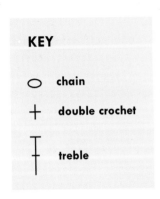

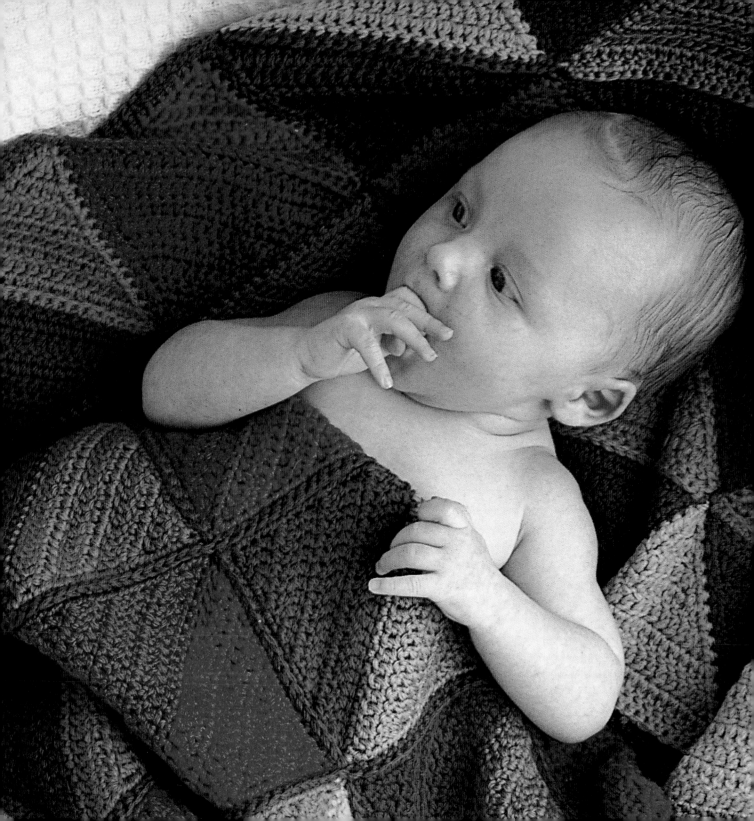

To Complete

Lay out the triangles with similar colours forming diagonals, to make 6 squares × 8 squares (or required number for size). This blanket had diagonals of blues, greens, yellows and pinks. Adding purples to blues and mauves to pinks, etc., makes up for any shortage of these colours and gives extra depth to the colour scheme. Join pairs of triangles into squares by using one of the 2 colours to crochet them together with dc right sides together (see page 18). Join the squares with dc wrong sides together (see page 18), using a dark colour.

Edging

Using a dark colour, right side facing and beginning at a corner, work a round of dc with 2 dc in each corner. Work 2nd round the same. Fasten off.

Idea: trim this blanket, or a plain one, with pairs of free-flying bobbles in several colours.

Materials

Brightly coloured Double Knitting yarn
3.50mm hook
Wool needle

To Make

Worked in rounds with RS facing but without joining rounds.

ROUND 1 Make 2 ch, work 6 dc in first ch.

ROUND 2 2 dc in each dc. 12 sts.

ROUNDS 3 AND 4 I dc in each dc, i.e. work 24 dc continuously.

ROUND 5 ★Insert hook in dc, yrh and draw loop through, insert hook in next dc, yrh and draw loop through, yrh and draw through all 3 loops; rep from ★ 5 times. 6 sts.

Cut yarn approximately 40cm, 16in from hook, thread end onto wool needle, remove hook leaving a long loop. Use some of remaining yarn to fill the ball. With the needle make a stitch over the outside strand of each of the remaining 6 stitches. Remove needle, insert hook in loop. Pull the thread up tight to gather the top, then make 10 ch. Fasten off, leaving an end for sewing on.

Inca hat

This type of strongly patterned hat with earflaps originated in the high altitudes of South America and makes very practical headgear for a cool climate.

Materials

Rowan 4-ply Cotton in 50g balls: 1 ball each magenta (A), navy (B) and turquoise (C)
2.00mm and 2.50mm crochet hooks

Size

To fit age 3–6 months (6–12 months)

Tension

24 sts and 25 rows to 10cm, 4in over dc using 2.50mm hook
Note: It may be necessary to use a hook one size larger to maintain tension over 2-colour area

Special Abbreviations (see page 19 for others)

dec 1 = decrease 1 st: [insert hook in next st, draw through loop] twice, yrh, draw through all 3 loops on hook
d dec = double decrease: as dec 1 but insert hook in next 3 sts, then draw yarn through all 4 loops

To Make

Worked from top in rounds with RS facing:
Using 2.50mm hook and A, make 5 ch, ss into first ch to form a ring.
ROUND 1 1ch, 11 dc in ring, ss to first ch. 12 sts.
ROUND 2 1ch, 2 dc in next st, [1dc in next st, 2 dc in next st] 5 times, ss to 1ch. 18 sts.
ROUND 3 1ch, 1dc in next st, 2 dc in next st, [1dc in each of next 2 sts, 2 dc in next st] 5 times, ss to 1ch. 24 sts.
ROUND 4 1ch, 1dc in each of next 2 sts, 2 dc in next st, [1dc in each of next 3 sts, 2 dc in next st] 5 times, ss to 1ch. 30 sts.
Cont to inc 6 sts on every round, working 1 st more before each inc on each round and working round 5 with A, rounds 6 and 7 with B, round 8 with C, rounds 9, 10, 11, 12 and 13 with A. 84 sts.
ROUND 14 With C, 1ch, 1dc in each st to end, ss to 1ch.

ROUND 15 With B, 1ch, 1dc in each of next 12 sts, 2 dc in next st, [1dc in each of next 13 sts, 2 dc in next st] 5 times, ss to 1ch. 90 sts. Cont to inc thus on alternate rounds until there are 96 (102) sts, then work straight until 24 (25) rounds have been completed.

NEXT ROUND Working with 2 colours (see pages 17 and 18) and in continuous rounds without 1ch at beginning and ss at end of round, ★ with A, 1dc in each of next 3 sts, with C, 1dc in each of next 3 sts; rep from ★ to end.

NEXT ROUND With C, 1dc in next st, ★ with A, 1dc in each of next 3 sts, with C, 1dc in each of next 3 sts; rep from ★ ending with C, 1dc in each of next 2 sts.

Cont thus, making each colour change 1 st along in the direction of work, until 15 (17) rounds of diagonal stripes have been completed. Work 4 (5) rounds in B. Fasten off. ★★.

Earflaps

Place a marker 7 (8) sts at either side of centre back, then 2 more markers, each 21 (23) sts beyond these.

With RS facing and using 2.50mm hook and B, work on one set of 21 (23) sts:

ROW 1 1ch, 1dc in each of next 20 (22) sts.

ROW 2 As first row.

ROW 3 1 ch, dec 1, 1dc in each of next 15 (17) sts, dec 1, 1dc.

ROW 4 1ch, dec 1, 1dc in each of next 13 (15) sts, dec 1, 1dc.

Cont to dec thus, 1 st in from edge and working 2 sts less in centre of every row, until 1ch, dec 1, 1dc, dec 1, 1dc has been completed.

NEXT ROW 1ch, 1 d dec, 1dc.

NEXT ROW 1 d dec. Fasten off.

2ND EARFLAP

On remaining set of 21 (23) sts work as first earflap.

Edging

With RS facing and using 2.00mm hook and B, work 1 round of dc along all edges, working 3 dc in point of each earflap.

With A, work 2nd round of dc, join with ss. Fasten off.

Make 2 small tassels with A and attach one to each earflap.

Idea: leave off the earflaps for a simple style.

Materials

Rowan 4-ply Cotton in 50g balls: 1 ball each navy (A), lilac (B) and turquoise (C)
2.00mm and 2.50mm hooks

Size

As Inca hat

Tension

As Inca hat

To Make

Work as Inca hat to ★★.
With RS facing, using 2.00mm hook and B, work 1 round dc along edge, then 1 round A. Join with ss. Fasten off.

Winter bootees

Bootees that look like socks are fun for indoors or outdoors. They're worked from the toe upwards and have the flap-style heel found in knitted socks from Eastern Europe.

Materials

Rowan True 4-ply Botany in 50g balls: 1 ball each Lime (A), Strawberry (B) and Navy (C)
2.50mm hook

Size

To fit 6–12 months
Sock foot approximately 12cm, 4¾in long

Tension

27 sts and 26 rows to 10cm, 4in over dc

Special Abbreviation (see page 19 for others)

inc 1 = increase 1 st: work 2 dc in next st

To Make

HEEL

Using A, make 2 ch.

ROW 1 Miss 1 ch, 7 dc in next ch, join in a ring with ss in ch. 8 sts. Work in rounds with RS facing working in the single back strand of each dc.

ROUND 2 1 ch, inc 1, [1 dc in next st, inc 1] 3 times. 12 sts.

ROUND 3 1 ch, inc 1, 1 dc in each of next 3 sts, inc 1, 1 dc in next st, inc 1, 1 dc in each of next 3 sts, inc 1. 16 sts.

ROUND 4 1 ch, inc 1, 1 dc in each of next 5 sts, inc 1, 1 dc in next st, inc 1, 1 dc in each of next 5 sts, inc 1. 20 sts.

Cont to inc thus on each round, working 2 more sts between first and 2nd incs and between 3rd and 4th incs, until round 9 has been completed. 40 sts.

Join with ss to 1 ch. Fasten off.

Idea: keep to one colour and add a lacy edging.

Materials

1 50g ball Rowan True 4-ply Botany in Strawberry
2.50mm hook

To Make

Using one colour only, work as three-colour socks to ★★. Mark this point with contrasting yarn. Cont as three-colour socks to ★★★. With RS facing, as before, work 20 rounds, 1 ss in next st.

EDGING

Working into both strands of each st, ★2 ch, 1 tr in next st, 3 ch, 6 tr around stem of tr just worked, miss 2 sts, 1 dc in next st; rep from ★, ending ss in first ch. Fasten off.

TOE
With B, work as heel but do not fasten off.

MAIN PART
★★ Cont with C.

ROUND 1 1ch, 1dc in each of next 39 sts.

ROUND 2 1dc in each of 40 sts.

Rep this round 12 times.

NEXT ROUND Press heel along incs to make a triangle. With RS tog and heel towards you, hold heel against main part. With C and working in back strand of each st as before, insert hook in first st of far side of heel and next st of main part, work 1dc. Cont to work together 1 st of heel with 1 st of main part until 20 sts have been completed. Fasten off.

Return to beg of rem 20 sts of heel, rejoin C and work 1dc in each of these heel sts, work 1dc in each of rem sts of main part to complete round. 40 sts. ★★★.

With RS facing, as before, work 11 rounds C, 5 rounds B, 2 rounds C and 5 rounds A. Ss in next st. Fasten off.

Tomato ball

The shaping of this realistic-looking tomato is so easy — it's simply a strip of chevron-patterned double crochet, sewn up and stuffed. It makes a ball that's easy to grab and soft to handle.

Materials

Double Knitting yarn in red and green
3.50mm hook
Polyester stuffing

Size

Circumference approximately 30cm, 12in

Tension

Approximately 20 sts and 25 rows to 10 cm, 4in over dc

Abbreviations (see page 19)

To Make

Using red, make 82 ch.
ROW 1 Miss 1 ch, 1 dc in next ch, ★1 dc in each of next 7 ch, miss 1 ch, 1 dc in each of next 7 ch, 3 dc in next ch; rep from ★, ending 2 dc in last ch.
ROW 2 1 ch, 1 dc in st below, ★1 dc in each of next 7 dc, miss 2 dc, 1 dc in each of next 7 dc, 3 dc in next dc; rep from ★, ending with 2 dc in ch. ★★.
Rep row 2 12 times.
Using green, work row 2 twice more. Fasten off.
STALK
With green, make 15 ch, miss 1 ch, 1 dc in each of 14 ch. Fasten off.

To Complete

Along green edge, fold each chevron in turn, and using green yarn stitch together the inside strand of each pair of stitches. Before sewing last chevron, insert stalk in centre and catch end securely. Join side seam, then fold and stitch chevrons at base, stitching the last one only after the ball has been filled with stuffing.

Idea: in yellow or orange the tomato becomes a melon or a pumpkin.

Materials

Double Knitting yarn in yellow or orange and green
3.50mm hook
Polyester stuffing

To Make

For a melon, using yellow, work as Tomato ball to ★★.
Rep row 2 14 times. Fasten off.
Or, for a pumpkin, using orange rep row 2 8 times. Fasten off.
Make stalk and complete as Tomato ball.

Resources

For more information on suppliers, contact the Rowan distributor listed below for your country:

UK
Rowan Yarns
Green Lane Mill
Holmfirth
West Yorkshire HD9 2DX
Tel: 01484 681881

Australia
Sunspun
185 Canterbury Road
Canterbury 3126
Tel: (61) 3 5979 155

Canada
Diamond Yarn
9697 St Laurent
Montreal
Quebec H3L 2N1
Tel: (514) 388 6188
www.diamondyarns.com

Diamond Yarn (Toronto)
155 Martin Ross
Unit 3
Toronto
Ontario M3J 2L9
Tel: (416) 736 6111
www.diamondyarns.com

New Zealand
Alterknitives
PO Box 47 961
Auckland
Tel: (64) 93760337

John Q Goldingham
PO Box 45083, Epuni
Lower Hutt.
Tel: (64) 4567 4085

USA
Rowan USA
4 Townsend West
Suite 8
Nashua
New Hampshire 03063
Tel: (1 603) 886 5041/5043
Email: wfibers@aol.com

For more information on suppliers, contact the Coats distributor listed below for your country:

UK

Coats Crafts UK
PO Box 22
Lingfield House, Lingfield Point
McMullen Road, Darlington
County Durham DL1 1YQ
Tel: 01325 394237
E-mail: consumer.ccuk@coats.com
www.coatscrafts.co.uk

Australia

Coats Spencer Crafts
Mulgrave North, Victoria 3170
Tel: (3) 9561 2298

Canada

Coats Patons
Toronto, Ontario M6B 1BB
Tel: (416) 782 4481

New Zealand

Coats Spencer Crafts
East Tamaki
Tel: (64) 9 274 0116

United States

Coats & Clark
8 Shelten Drive
Green SC 29650
Tel: (800) 243 0810

For stockists of Capricorn mohair:

UK

Capricorn Mohair Ltd
Black Cleugh Farm
Carrshield
Hexham
Northumberland NE47 8AE
Tel: 01434 345063
Fax: 01434 345178
E-mail: yarn@capricorn-mohair.com
www.capricorn-mohair.com

For stockists of Debbie Bliss yarns:

Designer Yarns Ltd
Units 8-10
Newbridge Industrial Estate
Pitt Street, Keighley
West Yorkshire BD21 4PQ
Tel: 01535 664222
Fax: 01535 664333
E-mail: lauren@designeryarns.uk.com

For stockists of Jaeger yarns:

Jaeger Handknits
Green Lane Mill
Holmfirth
West Yorkshire HD9 2DX
Tel: 01484 680050

THIS EDITION PUBLISHED IN GREAT BRITAIN

First published in Great Britain in 2002 by Collins & Brown Limited
64 Brewery Road London N7 9NT

A member of **Chrysalis** Books plc

1 3 5 7 9 8 6 4 2

British Library Cataloguing-in-Publication Data: A catalogue record for this book is available from the British Library.

ISBN 1 85585 993 9

Project manager: Claire Wedderburn-Maxwell
Instruction checker: Susan Horan
Editor: Eleanor Van Zandt
Designer: Sara Kidd
Jacket designer: Ruth Hope
Design conceived by: Luise Roberts
Photography: Sian Irvine
Art director and stylist: Ruth Hope
Chart Designer: Siriol Clary

With many thanks to Hilary Underwood who helped with the crochet and Susan Horan who checked the instructions; to the models and
their mothers: Skye Gentles and Lauren Weston, Polly and Katie Hardwicke, Gabriel Hall and Sian Irvine, and Maya and Varsha Sanderson; and
to Rachel Fraher at Silk PR and the White Company for providing the props.

Reproduction by Classic Scan Pte Ltd, Singapore
Printed in Hong Kong

Distributed in the United States and Canada by Sterling Publishing Co,
387 Park Avenue South, New York, NY 10016, USA